Both Alike to Thee

Canon Melvyn Matthews is the Chancellor of Wells Cathedral in Somerset where he has responsibility for the cathedral's programme of education and spirituality. He also oversees the Ministry of Welcome to the many visitors the cathedral receives. He was for some time the Senior Chaplain to Bristol University, but before that taught in the Department of Theology and Religious Studies in the University of Nairobi. More recently he was the Director of the Ammerdown Centre, an ecumenical laity centre near Bath. He has written a number of books, the most recent being *Rediscovering Holiness – The Search for the Sacred Today* (SPCK). He is married with three grown-up children and enjoys sailing.

D1424700

Both Alike to Thee

The Retrieval of the Mystical Way

Melvyn Matthews

Published in Great Britain in 2000 by
Society for Promoting Christian Knowledge
Holy Trinity Church
Marylebone Road
London NW1 4DU

The author and publisher acknowledge with thanks permission
to reproduce extracts from the following material:
T.S. Eliot: *Four Quartets*, 1943 © Faber and Faber.
Rainer Maria Rilke: *Sonnets to Orpheus*, translated by J.B. Leishman, 1964
© St John's College Oxford and Hogarth Press.
Paul Celan: 'Psalm' and 'Mandorla', in John Felstiner, trs:
Poet, Survivor, Jew 1995 © Yale University Press.
R.S. Thomas: *Counterpoint*, 1990 © Bloodaxe Books.

Biblical quotations are taken from *The New Revised Standard Version*
© 1971 and 1952, and from the *Authorized Version*, which is the property
of the Crown in perpetuity.

British Library Cataloguing-in-Publication Data

A catalogue record for this book is available from the British Library

ISBN 0-281-05030-9

Typeset by Wilmaset Ltd, Birkenhead, Wirral
Printed in Great Britain by
Redwood Books, Trowbridge, Wiltshire

Contents

Preface

This essay is an attempt to restate the mystical way for today's Christian. It is both a pastoral and an academic exploration. It is pastoral because Christians today desperately need to retrieve a spiritual life of great depth in order to remain faithful in a world which contains much moral and social disintegration. It is pastoral because the Church still remains very preoccupied with matters of liturgical and ecclesiastical reordering, a preoccupation which even after many years shows little sign of disappearing. Without 'a mystical life' all such reordering risks losing a theological direction. It is academic because in the recent past there has been a great deal of serious research into the mystical writers of the Christian tradition and into what they meant by what they said. Much of this remains little known within the on-going life of the Church. This research should have a considerable impact upon what we mean by 'spirituality', another preoccupation of the contemporary Christian. Readers familiar with this research will recognize my enormous debt to the monumental work of Bernard McGinn – which is still incomplete – and to the seminal writings of Denys Turner, Mark McIntosh and Grace Jantzen. These scholars have made a singular contribution to our understanding of what 'mystical theology' means which must be made accessible to the everyday life of the Church and somehow related to our pastoral situation. This book is an attempt to do that.

This task of popularization has been assisted, I believe, by a parallel set of developments in theology, again not well enough known about in the everyday life of the Church, namely the theological response to the development of postmodernism, some of which calls itself 'radical orthodoxy'. These writers have been bold enough to see the breakdown of modernism not as a threat to belief but as an opportunity to retrieve and restate the Christian tradition. If these two streams of thought are brought together, one concerned with historical research into what the mystical writers of the past said and meant, the other concerned with the way in which we can talk about faith in the face of the breakdown of modernism, and we see that they confirm each other, it becomes possible, I believe, in a very powerful way, to break the impasse of the present theological dilemma where conservative and liberal face each other over the barricades and by their infighting both misstate the tradition they seek to protect and confuse the outsider. A new synthesis can then be provided which enables faith to be retrieved and sustained in its fullness into the new millennium.

This book, therefore, is a broad exploration of the nature of the mystical life in the light of these recent intellectual developments and tries to relate these developments to the pastoral situation in today's Church. It tries to deepen the mystical life of God's people and to spell out the relevance for faith of the new understandings that have arisen within the walls of our colleges and universities. It is an exercise in bringing theology and spirituality together.

As with almost every writer in this field, I have had trouble with language. It is almost impossible to use the word 'mysticism' because in the popular consciousness this word is intrinsically bound up with the view that mysticism is some sort of ineffable and personal experience of union with the divine. As this is just what I think mysticism is not I have resorted to using phrases like 'the mystical way' or 'the contemplative consciousness' to express what I mean. Readers may find the use of such terms inexact, but I believe that the old terminology is now redundant and new words for the old reality must be found. I have also had problems (of course!) with God and gender, imperfectly resolved by using 'she' as well as 'he' in relation to God in an almost random manner in those situations where a personal pronoun cannot be avoided. I know this will enrage some as well as confuse others, but I take comfort in the fact that Julian of Norwich did the same. The chapter on 'The Re-enchantment of Action' first saw the light of day in a very different form in a single article in *The Merton Journal* (vol. 6, no. 1, Easter 1999), while much of Chapter 2, also in a very different form, appeared in the journal *Chrism* in the summer of 1998 (vol. 35, no. 2). I am grateful to the editors for permission to use that material.

I once complained to a friend that the pastoral activity of the church left little time for reading and writing. She replied that it was no better in the university and every writer had to write *in medias res*, 'in the midst of everything else'. Her comforting and goading words have been at the back of my mind throughout the writing of this book which, of course, has been done 'in the midst of everything else'. I would like to thank my colleagues here in Wells for their friendship and support but especially my wife June whose constant encouragement has, as always, been so invigorating. My grandson Thomas was baptized just as this book was finished and I would like to dedicate it to him, with much love.

Melvyn Matthews

1
'A deep, but dazzling darkness'

The mystical way is largely lost to the majority of Christian believers as an option within the mainstream life of the Church, but the recovery of the Church's life is dependent upon its retrieval. The moment at which the mystical way will open up as a possibility for the Christian believer has always been a moment of grace, but it has become increasingly necessary for the life and health of the Church, particularly the western Church, to allow that moment to emerge and to seek to create the conditions under which it will emerge. Even so, even when the Church has put into place the most sensitive programmes of spiritual awareness, and even when Christians become aware of the need to retrieve the mystical way, the basic requirement for its retrieval will be a moment of interior awareness of the inadequacy of the modern condition. In order to recover something of the necessity of the contemplative way believers have to come to a spiritual realization of the impermanence of modernity and of its innate capacity to fragment into unreality at the critical point. We need to rediscover how things are out of joint and to allow that sense of disjunction to grow within us. We have to grapple with a dissatisfaction with modern life and its attendant materialism. There has to be a deep and prayerful awareness of our dislocated condition and then there will arise within us a consequent desire, a true longing, a yearning even, to see that dislocation repaired and healed.

In the introduction to her translation of the writings of the Desert Fathers – those who, in the fourth century, left the conventional life of civilization and lived in simplicity in the Egyptian desert – Helen Waddell asks what harvest thought has reaped from what she calls 'the Desert fields'. She admits that at first sight the harvest is meagre

enough. The contribution to the philosophy of religion of those who
came to school in the desert is, she says, negligible. But she goes on
to say that there was one intellectual concept which the Desert
Fathers did give to Europe, namely eternity. 'These men, by the very
exaggeration of their lives, stamped infinity upon the imagination of
the West. They saw the life of the body as Paulinus saw it, *occidui
temporis umbra*, 'a shadow at sunset'.[1] And she quotes from the
Life of St Antony: 'The spaces of our human life set over against
eternity are most brief and poor.' Helen Waddell then goes on to
speak of the impact of Christianity on the pagan world in the most
startling and original terms:

> Paganism was daylight, Augustine's 'queen light', sovereign of
> the sense, rich in its acceptance of daylight earth: but Christianity
> came first to the world as a starlit darkness, into which a man
> steps and comes suddenly aware of a whole universe, except that
> part of it which is beneath his feet.[2]

She continues:

> In the world, hour by hour, the Desert Fathers taught us how man
> makes himself eternal. Starved and scurvy ridden as the first
> voyagers across the Atlantic, these finished with bright day and
> chose the dark. And, paradoxical as it seems, their denial of life
> on earth has been the incalculable enriching of it.[3]

To say 'Christianity came first to the world as a starlit darkness' is to
say something which startles the contemporary consciousness. We
have become used to thinking of the Christian faith in terms of the
light that it provides, the illumination that it gives to the mind and
soul. To understand it as a step into darkness requires a different
frame of mind, a change of attitude for which we are little prepared.
To then say that to make such a step actually provides an awareness
'of a whole universe' or to say that the denial of life means that it is
then incalculably enriched is to utter a hard saying. And yet, of
course, a moment's thought reveals not just that such words are
redolent of the words of Jesus ('He who denies his life will save it')
but also of certain elements of the Christian tradition which made
use of such negative language in later centuries. The use of the
phrase 'starlit darkness' conjures up Henry Vaughan's lines, 'There
is in God (some say) / A deep, but dazzling darkness ...' from his
poem 'The Night', and Helen Waddell anticipates by several

decades the current scholarly interest in the negative way of Christian mysticism and links the Desert Fathers to that tradition in a way which no other scholar had done before.

Equally important is Waddell's appreciation of the Desert Fathers' awareness of the stark and uncompromising demands which love makes in a secular world. Her words point us not just to the dark way to God of Dionysius, Eckhart and St John of the Cross, but also to the existentialist perception of the tedium of modern life, a perception which is to be found in figures as far apart as Pascal and Kierkegaard and has come to the fore in our own day among some postmodernist theologians. But even though she wrote nearly sixty years ago, and since then we have witnessed atrocities in Europe and elsewhere the like of which Helen Waddell could not have dreamed, we have still not absorbed the significance of what she said. She calls us to a darker and deeper journey than we have been willing to undertake and to a dissatisfaction with modernism which for some reason it has been almost impossible for contemporary faith to learn, in spite of the terrifying brokenness by which it has been surrounded.

But Helen Waddell's words startle us as much because western men and women have become beings who live on the surface of things. We may be dimly aware, certainly, that this condition is not that for which we were created and that there are powers unknown, hidden beneath the surface of our lives; but we are somehow unwilling or even unable to allow ourselves to be put in touch with those levels of existence. It is almost as if we believe that everything we cannot see is bound to be dark and destructive. We cannot believe that goodness awaits us. In the end we sail on the surface of the sea – aware that it is, after all, a very pleasant sea to sail upon. The primary external symptom of this dislocation between our surface existence and our deeper, inner being is the amassing of 'capital', things, possessions, insurances of one kind or another that we believe to be our own and to be inalienable and permanent. We place our trust in what can be known and possessed rather than in what cannot be seen. This may be called materialism, but materialism is not simply a matter of possessing or owning things – all of us, after all, own things and need to do so. Materialism is that condition of the mind or spirit whereby the person becomes attached to things, even good and necessary things, in order to be assured of identity. It is a condition which will not be cured by discarding possessions, by having or owning less. It will not be cured by giving things up if there is nothing to replace the void that will be left. Possession, or 'attachment' to use the ancient word, is a symptom of an inner dislocation of the spirit whereby the identity of the person concerned is in doubt. This dislocation is the true disturbance and it is this that prevents us from being in touch with the true sources not just of identity but also of right action in the world. It is also the primary symptom of modernism, the basic dis-ease from which we suffer. It is this which obscures our 'sight' of God and leaves us with collections of opinions rather than beliefs, conflicts rather than justice and peace, efficiency rather than gentleness and order, ambitions rather than contemplative prayer, continuous change rather than goodness or charity. in other words we are left with death.

There comes a point in the development of the Christian life when it becomes clear that another way is not only possible but necessary. It becomes clear that what has been good is turning to ashes and that instead of giving life it is in fact promoting death; instead of fulfilment it promotes the disintegration of personality. The rediscovery of the contemplative life by the Desert Fathers, or perhaps their realization that they must remain the guardians of the contemplative tradition, was associated with the growing conviction that their identity as persons was at stake and that the preservation of their identity required them to step into the 'starlit darkness' of which Helen Waddell speaks. If they wanted to remain human beings before God then they had to go elsewhere. 'These were men who believed that to let oneself drift along, passively accepting the tenets and values of what they knew as society, was purely and simply a disaster.'[4] The point of their dissatisfaction with life became the very point of their recovery of their own identity:

> The simple men who lived out their lives to a good old age among the rocks and sands only did so because they had come into the desert to be themselves, their *ordinary* selves, and to forget a world that divided them from themselves.[5]

A study of the Desert Fathers reminds us that a break with, or the expression of dissatisfaction with, modernity is actually a claim to recover our humanity; it is a statement about the necessity of saving what God has created and wishes to redeem from the false self which is being fabricated by the social compulsions of 'this world'. It is a statement that humanity, a truly fulfilled humanity with all the rich and bodily implications that entails, is only possible when exposed to the starlit darkness of God. What the Desert Fathers perceived was enlarged by the genius and imagination of Bernard of Clairvaux and those who wrote under his influence during the rise of religious humanism in the twelfth century. Bernard described the condition of the contemporary soul long ago in his treatise *On Loving God*:

> When the wandering mind is always rushing about in empty effort among the various and deceptive delights of this world, it grows weary and remains dissatisfied. It is like a starving man who thinks that whatever he is stuffing himself with is nothing in comparison with what remains to be eaten; he is always anxiously wanting what he has not got rather than enjoying what he has.[6]

According to Bernard all this happens because man 'ignores the glory which is within him'. The remedy, or at least the beginning of the remedy, is for the distracted soul to ask itself two questions. 'There are two things you should know: first, what you are; second, that you are not what you are by your own power.'[7] In answer to the first question Bernard believed that humanity is formed according to the image and likeness of God and is capable of living according to that likeness. Christ, the perfect Word of God, constantly calls humanity to conversion but the likeness to God which we possess has been concealed from us by our entrapment in the coils of this world. We live in a form of exile and have to return to our true selves if we are to be saved.

These insights have been affirmed by modern contemplatives. Henri Nouwen the Dutch writer is one such. Evocatively, he calls the condition we have been describing 'loneliness' and illustrates it with a quotation from the American Henry David Thoreau, who, almost certainly unwittingly, repeats the insights of St Bernard when he says:

> When our life ceases to be inward and private, conversation degenerates into mere gossip. We rarely meet a man who can tell us any news which he has not read in a newspaper or been told by his neighbour; and for the most part, the only difference between us and our fellow is that he has seen the newspaper, or been out to tea, and we have not. In proportion as our inward life fails, we go more constantly and desperately to the Post Office. You may depend upon it, that the poor fellow who walks away with the

greatest number of letters, proud of his extensive correspondence, has not heard from himself this long while.[8]

Another contemporary contemplative who describes this situation, and who was also an admirer of Thoreau, is the Cistercian monk Thomas Merton. He also repeats the comments of St Bernard but in clearly modern terms:

> Social life, so-called 'worldly life', in its own way promotes this illusory and narcissistic existence to the very limit. The curious state of alienation and confusion of modern man in modern society is perhaps more bearable because it is lived in common, with a multitude of distractions and escapes – and also with opportunities for fruitful action and genuine self-forgetfulness. But underlying all life is the ground of doubt and self questioning which sooner or later must bring us face to face with the ultimate meaning of life.[9]

All of this presents itself as profoundly alien to a modern mentality which understands the life it leads to be the result of progress and intelligence and which seeks fulfilment and enjoyment of whatever is offered. But is this the case? Is the 'starlit darkness' now lost in the broad daylight of reason and choice or does an alternative way still exist? Is modern man or woman actually capable of asking these questions?

A year or so ago there was a television programme which documented the effect being held hostage had on a number of people. Those involved were not the well-known personalities who had been held hostage, such as Terry Waite or Brian Keenan, but people who had been caught up in some of the terrorist incidents of the 1980s, and had been held in captivity for longer or shorter periods of time but with the prospect of being killed never very far away. One might have expected that such people had come out of captivity full of anger or resentment, feeling very negative towards the religious or political group that had held them, determined perhaps to seek redress or even revenge for what had happened to them; but in none of the cases shown in the programme was this so. As a direct consequence of his incarceration one man decided to mend his marriage, another decided to put his business on a more ethical footing, another, a rather hedonistic journalist, returned to the Church and went regularly on retreat, much to the puzzlement of his wife and family, and so on. The producer of the programme said that he could have repeated these stories many times over.

Reflection on these incidents – and on the effect that much longer periods of isolation had on Brian Keenan and to some extent John McCarthy – leads one to believe that whereas these periods of imprisonment were totally horrific, should never have happened and were not only an offence to humanity but also served nothing politically, they nonetheless had a very profound and long-lasting effect on those who were subject to them. It was almost as if they discovered themselves more, or were forced to abandon certain things about their lives that they knew they did not need or want.

In religious terms these people went through a stripping. It was not just that they were deprived of food or human contact or any of the normal things that one expects to have in western society, but that somehow they experienced a stripping of who they were. They had to reckon on being reduced, in personal terms, to the basic essentials of their being, as well as having to cope with living with the barest essentials of human comfort. They had to spend some time alone with themselves, so the question of who they really were became a central question – perhaps a question which they would not have had to face at all in normal western living. This 'stripping' is what the spiritual tradition has called an 'ascesis'. It meant that they had to lead the ascetical life without really wishing it upon themselves and so discover – perhaps even without realizing it – what those who deliberately seek the ascetical life wish to discover, that is, something about the essential nature of their humanity. The Desert Fathers were told, 'Stay in your cell and your cell will teach you everything.' Perhaps these people, who had been forced to 'stay in their cells' had learned, if not everything, then at least something, but in an involuntary manner. It is very interesting that at the end of his period of incarceration Brian Keenan is recorded as saying that he felt as if he was a combination of Rip van Winkle and Humpty Dumpty – someone who had awoken after a long sleep to find all of his parts in pieces before him, but that there were more pieces than he began with! In other words the loss of his liberty meant that he discovered things about himself that he was not previously aware of and so knew himself more fully and perhaps, in some ways, for the first time.

Reflection on these events will, I believe, help all of us to realize what dissatisfaction with modernity really means. What is happening here is that some people have been forced to reassess what it means to be modern. In the first place they had assumed, perhaps, that what western society gave them was what they as human beings had a right to expect as part of the fullness of life. They had assumed, perhaps unwittingly, that deprivation or limitation of the self was in direct contrast to what constituted a fulfilled human being or what a human being could properly expect if he or she was to be fulfilled. They emerged from their period of incarceration with this assumption directly challenged and with the seed planted in their consciousness that having everything does not necessarily make one a fulfilled person. They began to envisage the strange possibility that self-denial or voluntary restriction might be part of what a human being could choose or even needed to choose in order to discover, or rediscover, some hidden goals or aims in life. There is a danger, given the climate of the age with its emphasis on self-fulfilment, that the Church, if it talks about 'fulfilment' without due care and attention, could give the impression that what salvation really means is that we should lead a fulfilled life in the sense of being fulfilled by having everything that western society can give us, fulfilled in our chosen career patterns, full of life and complete health. Loss, or even the possibility of self-denial, is not accounted for. Such things are necessarily negative factors. Although this is something of a caricature there is, I believe, a grave danger that we could fall, at least to some degree, into this set of assumptions and so lose something of the vital essential characteristics of what the Christian tradition has meant by fufilment in Christ.

I think this needs some further analysis, because although it is true that modern society has apparently ruled out the question of loss or self-restriction or self-denial as part of what being a complete human being means, it is not simply a question which is settled by the reinstatement of self-denial as a means to full humanity, although that is surely part of what is needed. There is also the question of delusion. This is a more profound issue than the question of self-denial, important though that is, particularly in a political dimension where the relationships between the rich and the poor worlds are concerned. And this is so because what fulfilment came to mean to those who had been taken captive was not simply a capacity for self-denial but a capacity to relinquish what they felt was false about themselves or about the lives they had found themselves leading. Forced ascesis led to a voluntary awareness of the need for ascesis in order to be who they really were. This means that at least part of what it means to be fulfilled is the realization that human beings can be, and in modern society often are, in a state of delusion about who they really are and what they are for as people. Modern life appears straightforward, indeed looks very good, but it contains the most profound capacity for falsehood, for enabling people to generate identities, ways of being which they are best without.

If we are to be fully human I believe we have to embark on a journey where we accept the possibility, indeed perhaps the necessity, of being stripped of the unnecessary, of the self-generated images of the self with which we feed our ego-selves. There is the possibility, indeed the necessity, of embarking on a process of redemption, a journey which involves the stripping away of self-generated identities so that we may be released into the glorious liberty of the children of God. In other words there is a need to discern whether or not what humanity is offered as fulfilling is actually so and to leave behind what is not needed in order to live with God. It is this which has been the object of the spiritual life for so long. So if, at the beginning of this century, we want to recover our full humanity we must allow ourselves to be carried through a process of redemption – a process which is mirrored and enacted in the life of prayer and carried by the narrative of the community of faith. This process is one which takes us from the self-generated falsities of the ego-self, into what Henry Vaughan calls 'a deep, but dazzling darkness' and Helen Waddell calls 'a starlit darkness'. If we take that step then we will not only find that we have 'more pieces than we began with', but we will also find that we have stepped into the ancient contemplative tradition of the faith.

2

'A space within which God can act'?

God constantly speaks his word. To do so is to be God. God does not exist without speaking. Whatever exists does so because God speaks. Everything that exists is part of his speech. God does not speak and wait to see if we have understood, as if we were beings who could exist independently of his speaking and analyse what he was saying in an objective manner. Nor does he speak his word intermittently, rather he speaks constantly and speaks that constant word within his creation and within each human being. It is this speech which holds the creation in being. The very existence of the creation, the existence of humanity within that creation and then ultimately the appearance of Jesus Christ within that humanity, is his word and always has been his word. All is spoken into existence by God's word and Christ, as the Word of God from the beginning, is the very form, or essence, of creation. The human task, or rather the task which makes us human, is to recognize that our lives have become disconnected from that spokenness. In order to rediscover who we are we have to find that spokenness, to co-operate with it and to allow ourselves to be spoken by it. To do that is to recover our essential nature and to find God. Each person will know of moments when they have found that spokenness and allowed it to speak and so allowed themselves to be spoken and to become what, perhaps hesitantly, they perceived they might be. These moments are the rediscovery of reality since they are the moments when human beings recover their 'spoken' quality and can delight in being created and rest in the security that brings. Without that recovery human beings strive to find identity and security by their own speaking, by 'talk'. But human beings know that there is a choice between being spoken and existing by means of our own speech, by constant talking. There is a choice between listening and talking, between prayer and the wordliness, the 'modernity' of existing only by virtue of our own and other people's speech. Modernity is generated by the fear of silence.

The scriptures are the record of God's spokenness from the beginning. The Bible begins with the utterance of speech by God which brings the created universe into being from chaos. This speaking continues through the scriptural record until it climaxes in the spokenness of Jesus of Nazareth. In the Hebrew scriptures the people of God exist because they hear and respond to the word of God. When they hear and respond they flourish. When they do not hear or refuse to hear, they die. The psalmist understands the very existence of the created order to be a word from God such that not only the wild beasts themselves but also the provision of their food is 'spoken' into life by God.

> O Lord, how manifold are your works!
>   In wisdom have you made them all;
>   the earth is full of your creatures. . . .
> These all look to you
>   to give them their food in due season;
> when you give it to them, they gather it up;
>   when you open your hand, they are filled with good things.
> When you hide your face, they are dismayed;
>   when you take away their breath, they die.[1]

God speaks the fullness of his word in Jesus Christ, in whose own words this very same 'spokenness' is manifest. He speaks creative words to those who will hear and recreates them. In St John's Gospel not only is Jesus explicitly identified with the spokenness of God in the opening verses, but at a number of points through the narrative his activity, particularly his activity of healing, is related to the original speech of God the creator. In chapter nine Jesus heals the man who was blind from birth using words which relate his healing activity to the activity of God: 'We must work the works of him who sent me . . .'[2] He then uses the dust of the ground to create mud which he spread on the man's eyes. One commentator says:

> Jesus' healing constitutes the re-creation of the whole person. This is symbolically represented by the introduction of the clay

that is mixed with spittle, reminding the alert reader of the fact
that in Genesis God had first made Adam out of the dust of the
ground, when it had been softened by rain and mist (Gen. 2.5–7).
Or as Paul put it in a more theologically worded phrase: 'If
anyone is in Christ, he is a new creation' (2 Cor. 5.17).[3]

Although Jesus is explicitly identified as the Word of God in St
John's Gospel there is an implicit recognition of this role in other
places of the New Testament. Nor is such a recognition restricted to
the miracles of healing or recreation. In the Beatitudes, which form
part of the Sermon on the Mount in St Matthew's Gospel, it is clear
that those who are blessed or 'happy' are those who are totally open
to the spokenness of God within them and who do not attempt to fill
their own space with their own speech. Those who are empty and
content to be empty have recovered a capacity to be spoken and so
will be filled with the spokenness of God: 'Blessed are those who
hunger and thirst for righteousness, for they will be filled.'[4]

What the Beatitudes ask for is an attitude of mind and heart which
accepts the emptiness of things as a form of readiness, as a stage for
the activity of God rather than as a lack. Simon Tugwell in his
commentary on the Beatitudes makes this point constantly. He says:
'All our jockeying for position, striving to get ourselves into a more
influential and powerful place, is the bluster which comes from a
relative emptiness. ... We must learn to be incomplete, a space
within which God can act.'[5]

The central teaching of Jesus is a teaching about the need for self-
emptying so that we can be filled with the creative word of God.
God speaks this word from the beginning and the scriptures record,
in different ways, how humanity, how the people of Israel, and then
how Jesus, the ultimate representative of all of us, responds to that
speech within them. But Jesus is not simply a teacher of righteousness, he also enacts what he teaches and does so by means of his
own death. The death of Jesus on the cross embodies a moment of
self-emptying in order that he may perfectly embody the word of
God, and this self-emptying is elaborated theologically by the author
of the letter to the Philippians:

> Let the same mind be in you that was in Christ Jesus, who, though
> he was in the form of God, did not regard equality with God as
> something to be exploited, but emptied himself, taking the form of
> a slave, being born in human likeness. And being found in human

form, he humbled himself and became obedient to the point of
death – even death on a cross.[6]

Reflection upon this will enable us to see that what we have called
'Church' is the body of those who have recognized that they only
come to fullness of life by a response to the spokenness of God and
so allow themselves to be called, or called out, into existence. So the
Church is that place, that quality of life together, which enables
clarity of sight, which facilitates response and so enables those who
hear the spokenness at the heart of creation to refuse their own and
others' voices as means of identity and to step into the darkness and
clarity of God. To do this is to live the mystical life. The Church is
ultimately that place or that moment where human beings recognize
that they are empty and refuse to fill that emptiness with their own
dissembling, or their own sound and fury. Here hypocrisy and
dissembling are no more. Essentially the Church is that 'place'
where we find ourselves able to step into the darkness of God with
love and confidence. Each one of us must be brought by love and the
drawing power of love to that point where he or she is enabled to
make that step into the darkness of God with confidence and love.
Confidence and love are generated within the human soul when
confidence and love have been shown to it within the community of
faith. And it is significant that although the scriptures, both the
Hebrew scriptures and the New Testament, speak of the community
of God's people in theological language, using such terms as the
people of God and the Body of Christ, and speak of participation in
this community as necessary, this necessity is always a prelude, a
gateway rather than an end in itself. The goal is redemption by God,
not simply participation in communal life. The participation in
communal life is a sign of the necessity to participate in the glory
which is to be revealed at the end of all things. The Church therefore
is the place where God calls, it is the house within which the
knocking can be heard, for outside all that can be heard is the sound
of our own voices.

The truly mystical life is therefore a life which acknowledges that
we are separated from our true identity, and that this separation
derives from our striving for identity within this world. Being in the
world brings us a form of alienation. This is not to say that the world
is essentially evil, rather it is to say that our focus, our point of
vision, is distorted. Let Thomas Merton help us at this point. In one

of his essays Merton reviews the changes in relationship between the Church and 'the world' which have taken place and concludes that what is at stake is not a rejection of the world as such, not a turning from the created order, but rather a turning from the illusions which arise when 'the world' is given an identity of its own which it does not possess.

> When the world is hypostatized (and it inevitably is) it becomes another of those dangerous and destructive fictions with which we are trying vainly to grapple. And for anyone who has seriously entered into the medieval Christian, or the Hindu, or the Buddhist conceptions of *contemptus mundi, Mara* and 'the emptiness of the world', it will be evident that this means not the rejection of a reality, but the unmasking of an illusion. ... the way to find the real 'world' is not merely to measure and observe what is outside us, but to discover our own inner ground.[7]

So the mystical tradition asks us to believe that the effect of the world in which we live upon our souls is one of division; it separates us from our true selves and so in itself it does not bring fulfilment but risks death. Let us be clear, the mystical way does not condemn the world as such, but it has always been deeply and sharply aware of the delusory quality of worldly existence. Men and women are subject to this delusion and so can in certain circumstances lose their grasp upon who they really are. Religious life, existence within the community of the faithful, is intended to enable us to see how this is the case and to remove the scales from our eyes, to free us from this delusion. It is not intended to take us away from the reality of the world but to enable us to see the beauty of the world as it truly is, as it is in itself, and so to respect and care for what is, rather than seeing the world through the eyes of our own selfishnesses. The mystical way, from the Desert Fathers through to Thomas Merton, has held a deeply positive view of the Church as that 'place' where the Word of God knocks upon the soul and reforms it into its likeness. This is the place where our illusions can be lost and where we can rediscover our true humanity.

This emphasis on the spiritual essence of the Church has meant that the mystical tradition has been sharply aware of the way in which even the religious life can be assimilated to a 'modernity' which prevents the Christian hearing the insistent knocking of the Word of God. It is almost as if this tradition is particularly aware that there may come a point at which the practice of religious faith becomes no more than another distraction for the soul. If the significant moment at which the recovery of the mystical life becomes possible is a moment of nausea over the superficiality and materialism of modernity then it should also be clear that such a moment can and does occur deep within the life of the Church because the Church itself has become assimilated to this world. Contemplative reform movements, from the Desert Fathers, through the Cluniac and Cistercian reforms of the Middle Ages to the existentialist protests of the twentieth century and the rise of contemporary eremitism, have always pointed towards the ever attendant possibility that the Church itself might become ensnared in the modernity over against which it should be a sign of contradiction. The difficulty, in each generation, is recognizing that this can be and often is the case.

There are a number of stories in the sayings of the Desert Fathers which illustrate how they knew only too well how even the highest spiritual ideals could become an illusion. Even obedience to a monastic rule can obscure the purpose of the rule:

> A brother came and stayed with a certain solitary and when he was leaving he said, 'Forgive me Father, for I have broken in upon your rule.' But the hermit replied, saying, 'My rule is to receive you with hospitality and to let you go in peace.'

The difficulty lies in the truth that much of what is alleged to open the self to God can easily become part of the social compulsions of this world and actually hide the reality of God from our eyes. Even the pursuit of the life of prayer can become an obstacle, a work which in one sense has to be abandoned before God can be truly known. 'Yet another elder said, "If you see a young monk by his own will climbing up into heaven, take him by the foot and throw him to the ground, because what he is doing is not good for him." '

When we reach this point in our spiritual quest, when this truth becomes real to us then progress, real progress, becomes possible. Indeed, all the previous progress which the believer may think has been made up until that point will pale into insignificance when this dark moment has been understood to be a moment of opportunity and the threshold breached. The point will then have been reached when a forgotten Christianity is retrieved and we understand the faith to be 'starlit darkness' rather than 'queen light'. Then the believer enters a tradition which has existed from the beginning but which has by and large been neglected. At this point the dark night journey into the unknown reality of God can begin, childish things can be left behind and the believer become a space within which God can truly act.

In purely pastoral terms the arrival of the believer at this point can be readily explored. It is by no means unusual. The practice of the Christian life begins and continues in joy. It is a reality which we have accepted – usually gladly – but there may well come a point when we feel that its originally revealing power as a way to God has diminished or even dropped away altogether and has become an end in itself, a way which hides rather than reveals. We pray, practise the faith with good intentions and in good heart, knowing that this is what we have gladly chosen, but there may come an unease, an undefined sense that all is not well. This is often difficult to clarify or explain. Maybe it appears that the preoccupations of Christian discipleship within the Church are out of kilter with something larger, something undefined, a further and greater reality whom we have called God. Maybe prayer or personal relationships become difficult. Whatever it is the believer becomes aware that 'what is going on' and 'what really is the case' might be two different realities. We might feel that God should be the reality who speaks to us and whom we enjoy and celebrate, but we also, and at the same time, become aware that our grasp of who God is has somehow lost a great deal of its colour and life. We might have a vague sense in which the reality of God has become disguised behind the externals of Christian practice and belief while also being quite clear that the externals of Christian practice and belief must not be abandoned. We know that sort of radical rejection has been tried in the past and not worked and we do not wish to cut ourselves away from the sacramental sources of life, but we do know that they somehow need to be reconnected with the source of life which gave them birth. We need to find a way of bringing them back into relationship with the sources of their life, but do not always know how.

However, it is not always understood that this desire to be reconnected with the springs of our religious existence in the face of apparent aridity is not simply a matter of mental or intellectual dissatisfaction. A deeper disturbance is involved. What is at work here is a call, a call to the contemplative or mystical life. But once again deception is possible and it cannot be automatically assumed that as soon as a sense of aridity descends upon the soul then the call to the mystical life is present. There is no guarantee that a sense of aridity is in itself a sign that the starlit darkness of which we have been speaking is pressing upon the soul of the believer without other indications also being in place. It must be recognized that there are numerous situations or attitudes of mind which simply cannot make any claim to be an automatic gateway or entry point into the mystical tradition, and the mystical writers, particularly John of the Cross, make this clear. Among these are, for example, simple things like the struggle for truth, lack of understanding or dimness of vision. Nor can it be claimed that a simple sense of distance from God is a sign of a vocation to the mystical life. The sad but real condition of those who have lost touch with God through negligent practice, or the even sadder state of those who do not speak to God all week and then complain that they cannot hear what he has to say on Sunday, cannot be presented as indications of a need to move into mystical prayer. Some claim to have entered into the darkness of God when all that has happened is that they have refused to answer the knocking of Christ and are left with the sense that he has 'gone away'.

On the other hand, there are situations or conditions which are much more likely to be signs of the need to enter into the contemplative or mystical tradition. Most common is the condition of those believers whose lives have grown into God over many years but then have found that this growth has apparently stopped for no good reason. This religious seizure or freezing of the spirit will normally be accompanied by constant attempts to restart the process but all to no avail. Those who find themselves in this state are those for whom the darkness becomes more intense the more they press for answers. When this happens, and when advice has been sought and taken, then, but only then, would it be right to affirm that the gateway to the mystical way is being opened, as it were, in the darkness of the soul. But whereas it is clear that many will be deluded into thinking that such a moment has arrived, it is also clear that many more have abandoned a life of prayer just when they were on the brink of moving into the starlit darkness of which we have been speaking, simply through lack of good advice and through lack of awareness that the contemplative life is there for all who would enter into it. It is not a matter of waiting for ineffable experiences, rather it is a matter of waiting for that moment when no experiences

in prayer seem possible. The Church's preoccupation with 'light'
has prevented many from entering the mystical way and has kept
them in an infantilized spiritual condition for far too long.

The resolution of this dilemma, at a pastoral, ecclesiastical level,
is quite difficult because as soon as we enter into discussion with
others about these matters then that discussion too often becomes
abstract and academic and so unreal. Or, if not abstract and unreal,
then we find that attempts to resolve the dilemma on the ground
degenerate into anecdotal complaints about the institution, the
local vicar or minister, or result in unresolved and unresolvable
resolutions to do something different, with the result that people still
feel alienated or disturbed in an incoherent way. Some might
express their dissatisfaction by saying that the Church has to be
filled again with colour and life and evangelical bliss, and then move
into a more experiential form of worship and believing; but others
are somehow held back from this by caution or by fear or by
awareness of the dangers of experientialism or the New Age. Neither
way really resolves the underlying dislocation, indeed most apparent
solutions only appear to highlight the problem. But even then the
quest to become 'a place within which God can act' is further
delayed by the agendas of the contemporary Church. The inability of
the individual believer to arrive at the mystical gateway is
exacerbated by an institutional preoccupation within the Church
with a number of external factors. It is exacerbated by preoccupation
with the apparent loss of numerical strength in the churches and the
perceived need to repair that loss. This is not the place to enter into
arguments about the interpretation of statistics and whether that loss
is real or perceived. The effect upon the soul of the Church,
however, has been to induce a certain loss of self-confidence and a
somewhat frenetic reaching out to different ways of being so that
others may perhaps be drawn into the Church. It might then be seen
to be attractive in terms which those who are imbued with the spirit
of the age can understand. The effect of this on those who manage
the Church is to reinforce an activist and often ego-driven culture of
success. Already many of the clergy are driven by the need to
succeed. The demands of their ego-selves drive them to achieve and
be noticed. But it is already difficult for the clergy to keep this
natural and necessary part of their personality pattern in a proper
perspective because of the demands of their congregations. The
clergy are expected to be there, to provide answers, to chair

meetings, to have vision, to stem the tide of the disappearing worshippers, indeed to answer all of the questions which church members cannot answer for themselves and a few more besides. Inevitably these two forces, the demands of congregations and the ego-selves of the clergy, collude together and reinforce each other in the most powerful way. The result is that who the priest or minister really is becomes submerged beneath a false identity. This false identity is made up of a fatally strong combination of his or her own self-expectations and those of parishioners. At that point the real identity of the person concerned only surfaces briefly in anger with their family or in depression. A false person is present. Who the man or woman really is has gone. The deep sadness is that the man or woman who heard the call to life in the Church in the first place is not the person who is now active in the Church. That original self has been replaced by an ecclesiastical construct produced by a collusion between the ego requirements of the minister and the felt requirements, placed upon him or her, of the people he or she serves. In the present condition of the Church this collusion, severe as it is, is reinforced even further by a third force, that produced by the external demands of the institution itself, whether this be diocese or district or national committee. The institution only adds another set of requirements which assists in the inner collapse of the person concerned. But it is not simply the ordained leaders of the Church who are affected. So many others are driven by these forces that the Church is at the mercy of forces of activism which are only a symptom of its dislocation from its interior depths. What is needed is a strategy for the recovery of this person, a strategy for the recovery of the 'spoken', contemplative Christian, the one who is able to face the darkness of God without recourse to constructs such as an ego-self, the requirements of the congregation or the demands of the Church, but one who can face God and only God and be terrified, but also be burned and so become 'a place within which God can act'.

The phenomenon we are describing is not simply a pastoral phenomenon which can be treated by good advice and by re-organization of one kind or another. It lies far deeper than that. One of the failings of the modern Church is that it remains blind to the need for an in-depth analysis. It continues to treat symptoms instead of the real disease and to regard much of the solution in terms of shouting louder or pastoral reorganization. Indeed, part of the

difficulty is that it has for too long been regarded merely as a
pastoral phenomenon; the deeper theological malaise which under-
lies the pastoral evidence has been ignored. We are seeing in
pastoral terms the long-term results of a deeper disjunction between
spirituality and theology, which began its life some hundreds of
years ago and has only recently been seen to be of crippling effect.
Only the end, or the beginning of the end, of modernism as such has
enabled theologians to see exactly what the trouble has been all
along. Now that modernism is understood to be a potentially decep-
tive and so passing phenomenon we can see that its elevation into a
truth has been part of the disease from which we have suffered.

These questions are not simply pastoral ones, questions about the
pastoral condition of believers or the identity of the Church's
pastors. They present themselves in a pastoral form; at that level
they are serious enough, as we have seen, but they reach much
further. The dislocated condition of the believer might present itself
in a pastoral form, as if there is some personal need which requires
pastoral care, but the condition from which the believer is suffering
is the condition of the Church itself. It is the Church which needs to
recover a vision of its primary and its basic function. The integrity of
the evangelistic work of the Church requires a retrieval of the
mystical tradition. Christians need to hear the spiritual longings of
those outside the regular ecclesial communities, those who are
standing on its fringes and who are searching for a genuine
profundity of life. The integrity of the theological life of the Church
requires the same retrieval, as many theologians turn from what they
feel to be the vacuity of large parts of the liberal tradition to try to
answer the question of how and why the present separation between
theology and spirituality has occurred. In other words the pastoral
problems experienced within the Church will not be resolved until
the Church resolves to restore a contemplative core to its
evangelistic and theological activity.

3
A Colour-Blind Church?

As a university chaplain speaking to Christian students about our experience of God, I had enormous difficulty in introducing them to the apophatic mystical tradition, the negative way. Indeed I had enormous difficulty in introducing them to the mystical tradition full stop. Not only is this tradition, illustrated for example by the poetry of St John of the Cross or by the lyrical outpourings of Thomas Traherne, almost unknown to Christian undergraduates when they arrive at university, but it will be poorly understood and very much at odds with the experiences regarded by a large number of them as normative and desirable in today's religious climate. What is regarded as normative and desirable will be experiences of the presence of Jesus, of the saving power of the Holy Spirit, or perhaps the illumination brought by the message of scripture in a world darkened and confused by sin. Similarly, those talking about prayer to many Christian lay people will find it difficult to demonstrate that the experience of the absence of God in prayer can in any way be regarded as a positive factor, in spite of the massive evidence in scripture and the Christian tradition that this is and has been the case. There is a contemporary insistence that the light of Christ must always be with us and that if it is not then the fault lies with our capacity to see.

These experiences are only further evidence of the dichotomy between the self-understanding of large sections of the contemporary Christian Church and the apparent spiritual longings and desires of the so-called secular world. While much of the Church has, broadly speaking, allied itself to a way of talking about the faith which emphasizes the light and truth brought by Christ, the secular world is still fascinated by a spirituality of mystery and is unable or hesitant to accept the apparently clear truths of the message the

Church wishes to impart. Whereas a large section of the contemporary Church appears to be increasingly content with the pre-packed 'truths' of a certain type of Christian exposition, the modern secular imagination, when it turns to religion, is more willing to linger with the different dimension to religious awareness afforded by things like icons, candles, silence, Gregorian chant and hints of mysticism. One begins to wonder whether the Church has too easily adopted the rational vistas offered by the modern world, vistas which plainly know the truth about what used to be called 'the mysteries of the faith', and is almost too confident in its ability to prove these mysteries true to others; whereas the starved imagination of the secularized and postmodern individual hesitates to turn away from the unresolved categories of the poetic and religious, what Keats called our 'negative capabilities', capabilities which some forms of institutional Christianity appear to have abandoned.

Among those who are not formal believers, there is an awareness that the spiritual traditions of the Church contain a mystical or contemplative path and that this way might well have something to say to those who, aesthetically or intellectually, find the current emphases of the Church difficult to sustain. A recent television programme included a number of sequences filmed in one of our great cathedrals and illustrated the space, silence and beauty of the building and the spiritual qualities of the activities it contained. The commentator, a contemporary novelist, said, 'When this cathedral was built people would have shared a vivid spiritual life. Our society has lost that almost completely.' She went on to say, 'If this wasn't the apologetic old Church of England we'd be stunned by this place. If this was a Buddhist temple or a Muslim shrine we'd be enormously impressed by the combination of such beauty and spirituality.' Such remarks are very revealing, implying as they do that the Church of England risks obscuring its own depth by its current image, almost saying that the casual disregard of our own spiritual traditions leads us to recognize the spirituality of other religions long before we are able to acknowledge the inherent spirituality of our own.

A similar point is made by those who attempt to keep alive an emphasis upon the use of beauty and imagination in the life of the Church. One of them, the Bishop of Oxford, says:

As with the experience of beauty in nature, unless the Christian faith has an understanding and place for the arts it will inevitably fail to win the allegiance of those for whom they are the most important aspect of life. For they will see in the Christian faith only what strikes them as flat, moralistic and platitudinous compared to the haunting depths of Mahler or *King Lear*. Unless the experience of beauty in nature and the arts is encompassed and affirmed the Christian faith will seem to have nothing of interest or importance to say. This is not, however, just a tactic to win the allegiance of the lost. The fact is that God is beautiful and the Church is hiding this.[1]

Such a comment complements the remarks of the novelist about spirituality in the television programme quoted above, and reinforces the view that there is a perceived difference between the contemporary stance of the Church – a stance which appears to hide or limit or even be ignorant of the spiritual tradition to which it is heir – and the longings of the secular world which asks those of faith to return to a confidence in the spirituality of their past and recover a security in the mystical or contemplative traditions which they risk hiding from themselves.

Those concerned to retrieve the mystical or contemplative life of the Church would want to echo and then enlarge the last sentence of the Bishop of Oxford's words by saying, 'The fact is that God is beautiful *and invisible* and the Church is hiding this.' For the truth is that the Church needs to recover its knowledge of, its confidence in and its growth within an understanding of the invisibility of God, together with the innate attractiveness of that invisibility, if it is to relate to the world in which it is set. Its ownership of the spiritual tradition which contains that negative awareness appears to be lost, while the contemporary world is there, standing on the sidelines, asking Christians to recover that tradition and its significance in order to allow them to re-enter the sacred space with confidence. The Church does no service to its own integrity, let alone to the understanding of its life which others have, if it does not seek to respond to this situation. We are being recalled to the dark way.

I once began a radio broadcast, one of those which go out at a few minutes before the news each morning, with the words 'God is invisible'. None of my colleagues remarked upon this except my near neighbour, the Orthodox priest, who stopped me in the street to enthuse over those three words. He had never heard an Anglican priest speak of God in those terms before, and yet, he said, this is the

Orthodox tradition. But, he continued, this is also what we ought to be saying to those who come into our churches from time to time and then go away. We do not know what God is like in his entirety, we cannot see him in his completeness. We should be overwhelmed by his immensity rather than talking about him as if we can see him directly in front of us. We should be more often silent or more often ecstatic. Then people outside will understand us better. At the moment we spend too much time talking to our own people in terms which are determined by us rather than by the real demands of the world in which we live.

But it is not only the outsider, or the secular novelist intrigued by the mystical qualities of our great cathedrals, nor the fragmented consciousness of the postmodern individual, who is recalling the Christian Church to its mystical roots. A number of modern theologians are beginning to remark upon the separation that has arisen between theology and spirituality. In fact, many modern theologians who disagree in very serious ways about the remedy for this situation actually agree about its reality. In broad terms, what is being said is that through the earlier years of Christian history there existed a hegemony in which thinking and devotion, theology and spirituality, speculation and prayer were held together in an intrinsic relationship. There was no divorce between the desire for intellectual clarity and the desire to meet the spiritual needs of the people, no divorce between a life of scholarship and speculation and a life of prayer. Scholars differ as to the dating and indeed the causes of the disappearance of this hegemony of thought but there is broad agreement that much of our theological malaise in the twentieth century has been due to its disappearance. One of the most thorough and contemporary studies of the decline of this unity between theology and spirituality and the need for its retrieval in the modern age is to be found in the work of a North American theologian, Mark McIntosh. He shows that during the period of the Middle Ages the conditions under which the unity between spirituality and theology had been maintained became more and more difficult to sustain:

> During this period of the rise of scholastic theology there were also shifting trends in Christian spirituality that made it harder for the two realms of life to communicate, let alone nourish each other. In much later medieval spirituality, the self comes to be construed more and more in terms of its inner life, its experiences

and affectivity. Thus, participation in the mystery of Christ is likely to seem all the more purely a matter of the 'private and particular'. Coinciding with the growth of scholasticism, medieval spirituality's intensifying focus on individual experience and affectivity gave rise to a spiralling mutual distrust between spirituality and theology that lingers even today.[2]

McIntosh is not the only student of the history of Christian spirituality to come to these conclusions, although, as we shall see, he is one of the few who try to provide a way forward in an attempt to retrieve the unity which we have lost. Some time ago Rowan Williams, in a seminal study called *The Wound of Knowledge*, pointed out that the late Middle Ages had seen the growth of a profound distrust of the capacity for human reason to attain religious knowledge and saw this distrust reinforced by the views of William of Occam and Duns Scotus. But however this split came about and however it is dated, it is generally agreed that by the time of the Reformation it only needed a figure such as Martin Luther to lock religion firmly away in the locker of human piety, to discard the key of reason and then, in a *coup de grace*, call upon the rising nation states of Europe and the power of the princely states to act as gaolers to the death of creative links between theology and spirituality. If the Reformation did not complete the divorce then the Enlightenment of the eighteenth and nineteenth centuries was free to do so. The twentieth century has seen the legacy of this division affect the thinking of everybody, so that religion has become an almost entirely private and personal affair concerned with individual experience, while science has reigned undisturbed by thoughts of a relationship between it and God.

Not only does such a divide result in the privatization of religion, it also opens the floodgates of secularism. If religion is now understood to be a private pastime then the pursuit of reason, which plainly brings so much in terms of scientific and industrial advance, is unfettered and becomes godless. Reason becomes its own determinant, its control is in its own hands. The final result of the eighteenth-century Enlightenment was simply to detach reason from religion in a final and determinative manner so that the secular nation state, governed by the light of reason alone, could emerge. The result is that there is not only a total disjunction between reason and experience in the modern nation state, but there is a similar dichotomy within the life of the Church between thinking about God and experiencing God, that is, between theology and spirituality, between the pursuit of the active life of the Church and attention to the reality of God, between teaching and prayer, between management and worship. So in both Church and state, in civic and religious life, there is a total disjunction between faith and reason, in which reason is understood to be about progress and development, and religion is understood to be personal and reasonably harmless – although many have come to dispute even that – provided it is kept in the private domain.

Mark McIntosh, however, shows how this separation is in fact crippling both the academic and theological task of the Church and its spiritual life and says that neither will flourish properly until they are both brought back into a proper relationship with each other. There is a growing consciousness among some of the Church's theologians that in order to interpret the tradition properly the links between theology and spirituality have to be restored. We have to move back, beyond an attempt to speak of the truths of the faith simply in rational terms, an attempt which permits rationalism to determine theology, to a way of speaking about the faith which allows the fullness of the tradition, including the mystical, to have a proper voice. This, of course, is a distinct shift in the approach to theology from that which has obtained in the recent past. It is an approach which recognizes the fallibility of the secular and which attempts to reinstate a theological framework as that which is able to interpret the world. It sees the present implosion of modernity and the arrival of what is now called postmodernity as a supreme opportunity for the reinstatement of the primary task of theology, that is, to interpret the whole world as being ultimately under God and only finally comprehensible when the transcendent reality of God is fully recognized. If everything is fragmented, then the opportunity is provided for a coherent and inclusive view. In a clarion call for the reinstatement of this position these theologians say:

> For several centuries now, secularism has been defining and constructing the world. It is a world in which the theological is either discredited or turned into a harmless leisure-time activity of private commitment ... And today the logic of secularism is imploding. Speaking with a microphoned and digitally simulated

voice it proclaims – uneasily, or else increasingly unashamedly – its own lack of values and lack of meaning.

They go on to set out their own programme for the recovery of the theological:

> What emerges is a contemporary theological project made possible by the self-conscious superficiality of today's secularism. For this project regards the nihilistic drift of postmodernism as a supreme opportunity. ... in the face of the secular demise of truth it seeks to reconfigure theological truth.[3]

Or, as one of them says in direct terms:

> I wish to argue that with postmodernism God emerges from the white-out nihilism of modern atheism and from behind the patriarchal masks imposed by modernity's secular theology. ... In the postmodern cultural climate, the theological voice can once more be heard.[4]

The writer of those sentences, Graham Ward, then goes on to point out how so many of the so-called postmodern theologians have drawn inspiration from 'concepts, metaphors and texts culled from before the onset of modernity'. These include a considerable interest in the mystical tradition in general and the negative way of Pseudo-Dionysius and Eckhart in particular. These contemporary theologians would say that 'hiddenness' is an acceptable and necessary category in the study of theology. One of them writes: 'The task of the theologian must not be to turn away from the painful and ecstatic silences or the un-looked for words of mystical speech.'[5]

Mark McIntosh, whose words these are, makes the intriguing suggestion that the Church has been colour-blind for the last hundred years or so and is only now able to recover some of the depth and colour to its thinking that it had in a previous age. He suggests we make a comparison between what has happened to the way we talk about God and an imagined event in the artistic world. Suppose, he says, that all the artists of the world suddenly went colour-blind. All of their works would continue to be marvels of artistic construction, of balance and movement, but we would feel that something absolutely vital was now missing. The rest of us, perhaps regarded as amateurs, would feel that the artists had lost touch with something, that mysterious language which we really need for expressing what is real. But, he says, when we tried to tell the artists this then they derided us, saying that we had not understood true art or were hopelessly undeveloped in our taste.

> My suggestion is that something analogous to the artists' colour-blindness has happened to theology. And when theology loses its sensitivity to the 'colours' of spiritual practice and mystical speech, when it tends to overlook them as mere religious kitsch, it is gradually losing touch with that mysterious language by which humanity and the ultimately meaningful have access to each other and are able to enter into dialogue.[6]

But, there are serious problems with the interpretation of mysticism. The difficulty is that once you start to use the term 'mystical' or 'mysticism', as McIntosh does, many people, especially perhaps those from within the liberal tradition of the Church, begin to lose interest. They naturally assume that you are talking about so-called 'mystical experiences', where the person experiences some sort of alleged union with the divine, and that, of course, is understood to be suspect, and so lack of interest sets in. Even as recently as twenty or thirty years ago the mainstream church consciousness was broadly ecumenical and practical in temper. Co-operation, good works and service, at home and abroad, was the order of the day. There was a plain piety about, which eschewed experience and elevated action. These were the days when Dag Hammarskjöld, then Secretary General of the United Nations, wrote in his diary, 'In our day the road to holiness inevitably lies through the world of action.' Mystical experience was regarded as something of a private matter or of no real importance. Indeed mystical experience was even thought to be risky, an indulgence which might warp or disturb the judgement of sensible, action-oriented Christians. In 1987 the Doctrine Commission of the Church of England wrote:

> Those who believe in God ... testify to a variety of 'religious experiences' from a general sense of the holy or numinous, on the one hand, to a sensation of being directly addressed by a transcendent being, on the other. Not only is such experience open to the charge of being subjective, it also appears to be unequal if not haphazard in its distribution. Many profound believers claim

to be ignorant of it; many powerful experiences fail to result in a solid faith ... such experience is often ambiguous.[7]

The deeply sceptical tone of those remarks towards 'religious experiences' was not uncommon at that time. But there has been, over recent years, a realization that the 'experiences' of which the Doctrine Commission spoke are not so haphazard or as ambiguous as was once thought. We have become much more aware of the importance of religious and mystical experience, and much more aware that it is more widespread than we had recognized. There is even hard evidence that this is the case. The Alister Hardy Research Centre, which was set up in the late 1970s to research religious experience, conducted a large number of interviews and collected a great deal of evidence from people in all walks of life and of all faiths and none to show that mystical experience was not far from ordinary people. What is clear from the evidence is that most people *do* have religious or even deeply mystical experiences, which, when they have had a chance to reflect on and think about them, they value and live by. What people do *not* do is relate these experiences very closely to church life, nor do they interpret them well. The sceptical mood has prevailed for so long that the necessary tools of interpretation are simply not present within the community at large, and the Church has adopted attitudes similar to those of the Doctrine Commission for so long that it is not able to help. The consequence is that these 'experiences', if that is what they are, and there is some doubt about that, are uninterpreted and unintegrated either into the life of the individual or into the life of the Church as a whole. The institutional life of the churches and religious experience is, normatively speaking, disconnnected.

However, there are signs of a shift in attitude. Parts of the scholarly community are becoming aware that there is fertile ground here for academic enquiry. Scholarly studies of the Christian spiritual tradition are becoming more commonplace. Courses of study of the mystical tradition are becoming easier to find, and, what is more, answering an obvious hunger. There is a growing awareness of the restrictions that modernism has placed upon our use of language. A number of contemporary theologians are now saying that human beings in the modern age, who speak about matters of faith either in purely rational or in purely experiential terms, have lost that capacity people had in earlier times to speak of God in ways which included both the rational and the experiential because they knew that as human beings they were fulfilled by attention to what were called 'the sacred mysteries', by attention to the hiddenness of God within the whole of the scriptural and liturgical activity of the Church. There is a movement afoot within the Church to recover from colour blindness and to begin a process of once more offering an entrancement, a re-enchantment of the bourgeois mind, as a central element not just in the way in which we speak to others about God but also in the expression of our own self-understanding and in giving voice to our own integrity.

We shall be referring to this body of scholarship in the course of this book. In many ways the point of this book is to make this work accessible to the general reader in the Church and to consider its implications for the Church and its spirituality in the modern world. The point to make at this juncture is that once it becomes clear that mysticism is not, or at least was not in the Middle Ages, regarded as a matter of private and personal experience limited to the few, then this opens enormous possibilities for the life of the Church, for the development of its own spirituality and, of course, for dialogue with the modern world. The field is then clear for a re-examination of the role that mysticism can play in the life of the Church as a whole. This essentially frees mysticism from the private and from the esoteric, whence it had been relegated since the days of scholars such as William James and Evelyn Underhill, and rescues it for the mainstream Christian. The mystical way becomes no longer the preserve of the few who are privileged by particularly intense experiences; the path is open for a retrieval of mysticism in the Church as being part of the common property of the faithful.

These pages are written in the belief that the contemplative and mystical traditions of the Church have not disappeared entirely but have simply gone underground and are awaiting retrieval by the Church that gave them birth. The time is ripe for their retrieval, not only because it is clear on examination that the style of faith being practised in the Church today has inherent and almost invisible fault lines which are beginning to become apparent, but also because mysticism itself is meanwhile being retrieved from the mists of personal experience whence it was sent by the armchair theologians of the Victorian age. The postmodern fragmentation we now face enables us to recover the lost nature of the mystical life and to bring it once more centre stage so that the Church can speak once again to the people of the age whose awareness of and hunger for the mystical way is stronger than we realized.

But there is even more to it than that. There is more to the disappearance of mysticism from the life of the Church than a theory about the undue influence of the Enlightenment or the misinterpretation of medieval texts. These things are undoubtedly true, but still we know that there is more to it than that. We sense that however complete the historical analyses we may make about the shifts in theological thinking, or however clear we are about the shifts in linguistic expression of theological truth which have occurred since the time of Eckhart or John of the Cross, and there is no doubting their importance, there is still something else. However ripe the times may be for a recovery of mystical awareness of God, why we lost that awareness is not totally explained by the movements of history or the development of the Church. There is still something else, something to do with us and our understanding of spirituality, something to do with us and the way we believe in God, something to do with our own faithlessness. There is, simply, the question of how we believe and what sort of God we believe in. What has happened is that we have turned the focus of our attention away from the deep and dazzling darkness of God and the immensity of his reality and settled, in our hearts and minds, for something much, much less, namely a God who is no bigger than we can cope with. We have in fact settled for the comfortable. We have settled for a comfortable pastoral practice, we have settled for a comfortable analysis of the human person, and we have settled for a God we can talk about. In each case we have drawn back from the darkness, or, to use the words of the German poet Rilke, we have been aware that beauty is but the beginning of terror, and have shaded our eyes. In each case our Church, our self-understanding and our theology have been diminished. We are working with blunted tools and are using models of understanding that restrict or reduce our capacity to be a pastoral force, to understand ourselves and to speak of God. We could have so much more. So the task is to re-enchant the bourgeois mind and heart. First we have to re-enchant our awareness of ourselves, our self-understanding, and release ourselves from the grip of a view of the self which declines to live with an openness to the beauty of God. We have to retrieve what some would call a bridal anthropology, a view of the self as bride rather than director. We have to re-enchant our ways of talking about God and learn to use poetic discourse in both our worship and our theology as a matter of course. And we have to re-enchant our pastoral practice so that our clergy may enter into a mystical heritage which has been waiting for their return. Let us deal with each of these in turn.

4
'My Beloved Spake...'
The Re-enchantment
of the Self

A drive from the city where I live towards the north coast of
Somerset will bring you round the edge of the Quantock Hills and,
as you drive along the coastal plain before you climb once again on
to the empty spaces of Exmoor, you will cross several streams
flowing out of the isolated but fertile valleys which reach up into the
high land to the south. It was to one of these valleys, with its river,
that a group of monks came some eight hundred years ago. They
cleared the land and settled there, building their characteristically
simple monastic church and cloister, and lived a life of praise, of
prayer, love and remembering until they were forced to leave nearly
four hundred years later. They were Cistercians, and the remains of
their abbey can still be seen with its large and impressively simple
dormitory, which has a door at the end which once led down to the
monastic church but which now opens into emptiness. Not just the
thinking but the whole way of life of these monks was deeply
influenced by Bernard of Clairvaux. Any casual visitor to Cleeve
Abbey, or any other Cistercian foundation, should walk slowly
around these monastic remains asking a number of questions. What
was it that drew so many good men to this way of life at that time in
history and what was it that sustained them? The answer will be
found by looking at the style of life which they led and then asking
what it was that sustained that life, for their life was not just a life of
prayer and enclosure. The Cistercians were not only among the
greatest reformers of monasticism itself, at least as it had developed,
but they also challenged the secular, feudal system of agriculture. In

the Cistercian reform abbots became more responsible to each other, thus they reordered the way in which monasteries related to each other. The system of farming which they instigated, using 'granges' and lay brothers as participant farmers, challenged the feudal system. These reforms were therefore not simply reforms based upon a more rigorous observance of the Benedictine Rule, or the pattern of liturgical observance, but they were reforms which went a great deal further and were able to do so because they were dependent upon a richer theological and anthropological perspective. They drew upon a new-found understanding of the nature of the human person. Friendship and mutual love became more important than simple monastic order and discipline.

Bernard and his colleagues believed that human beings had not lost the imprint of the image of God upon their soul but that this imprint had become deeply obscured and needed to be called out of the darkness into which it had slipped. It needed to hear once again the call of the beloved. At one point, not long after he had begun his monastic career, Bernard was ill and spent some time convalescing in the company of William of St Thierry. The two men talked together of the Song of Songs, a favourite book of medieval monasticism. In 1135 Bernard began a series of sermons on the Song of Songs which he continued until his death in 1153. The Song of Songs is really a cry of erotic longing by the lover for the beloved. It contains a female voice, that of a dark and beautiful woman who calls in the night for her lover. There is a male voice, the voice of one who is fair and ruddy, whose head is as the most fine gold and who has 'lips like lilies dropping sweet smelling myrrh'. These voices call for each other and search for each other through the city where they dwell. But the Song also contains an element of unknowing, a search which is unfulfilled, and the combination of erotic longing and lack of fulfilment, together with the richness of the imagery used, make the Song of Songs one of the most evocative love poems of all time.

> My beloved spake, and said unto me, Rise up, my love, my fair one, and come away. For, lo, the winter is past, the rain is over and gone; the flowers appear on earth; the time of the singing of birds is come, and the voice of the turtle is heard in our land ... By night on my bed I sought him whom my soul loveth; I sought him, but I found him not.[1]

From very early in the Christian tradition this great poem was understood to be an allegory of the love between God and the soul, but it was Bernard and the Cistercians who took this allegory to the greatest heights. Bernard not only sees the soul as lost within the entanglement of this world, but also not fully itself until it reaches up and is kissed by the Bridegroom. Then we shall know even as we are known and be drawn into the embrace of God. The Song opens with the call, 'Let him kiss me with the kisses of his mouth', and Bernard writes:

> Listen carefully here. The mouth which kisses signifies the word which assumes human nature; the flesh which is assumed is the recipient of the kiss; the kiss, which is of both giver and receiver, is the person which is of both, the Mediator between God and man, the man Jesus Christ.[2]

Bernard then continues to expound the kiss of the word of God in terms of three kisses: the kiss of the feet, the kiss of the hand, and then, finally, the kiss of the lips when we shall be made whole.

> My heart rightly says to you, Lord Jesus, 'My face has sought you; your face, Lord do I seek'. In the morning you showed me your mercy. When I lay in the dust to kiss your footprints you forgave my evil life. Later in the day you gave joy to your servant's soul, when, with the kiss of your hand, you gave him grace to live a good life. And now what remains, O Good Lord, except that now in full light, while I am in fervour of spirit, you should admit me to the kiss of your mouth, and grant me the full joy of your presence.[3]

Bernard points out that there must be some points of likeness between our knowledge of our selves and our knowledge of God or else we could not learn from one about the other, as God intends us to do. God does not come to some wretch who is in total darkness; rather the darkness is the darkness of exile, the human soul is in the land of unknowing, but it is a land where it ought not to be, a land for which it was not made and it must discover that its birthright is elsewhere, that it was made for something else. Bernard's understanding of human nature is that it is made by and for love, but humanity has lost sight of what it was made for and must be brought home. The monastery, or at least the Cistercian monastery, is where this journey home can take place. As Bernard McGinn says in his study of this period:

In the history of mysticism, the twelfth century is unsurpassed in its exploration of the experience of the spousal love of Christ. *Brautmystik* as it is called in German. Bridal mysticism, however, was part of a wider concern for the *ordinatio caritatis*, the effort to energise and harmonise all the powers and relationships of individual believers and the whole body of the church toward the love and enjoyment of God, the true and final goal ... The twelfth century mystics saw the ordering of love not as an attempt to control and stifle love, but as the only way to allow it to develop the fullness of its power and passion.[4]

Bernard believed that the human soul could only regain its truly passionate nature by turning its gaze towards God. There is, therefore, in his anthropology an openness towards the divine which human beings have themselves closed or allowed to be closed by their preoccupation with sin. The human soul is properly compared to the Bride, while Christ the Word of God is the Bridegroom, and the process of redemption is a process of transformation from glory to glory. So it will come as no surprise to know that one of Bernard's favourite texts was a verse of St Paul: 'All of us, gazing upon the Lord's glory with revealed face, are transformed into the same image from glory to glory, as if by the Spirit of the Lord.'[5]

Much of Bernard's understanding of humanity has been lost because we are more recently convinced that identity is given to humanity by means other than the search for the Bridegroom through the night. Desire – which might be a modern translation for Bernard's use of the word love – has become a private, sexual word, or has been replaced as a word which describes the central mechanism of the human person by words like reason or action or absurdity or by some combination of all three. Bernard's openness to the transcendent has been replaced by closed systems of thought. Christians themselves have not bothered to have a view about human nature and how it functions or what its central driving force might be, regarding that as a task for philosophers rather than theologians, and simply asserting various theological truths without accompanying those thoughts with any anthropology. Indeed, Christian or even religious anthropology has virtually disappeared from the western mind set. Part of the reason for this is that what little Christian anthropology survived the Reformation has since faced a two-pronged attack. At some point in the seventeenth century theologians, and not just Protestant ones, lost their confidence in the ultimately divine origin and destiny of human nature, while philosophers moved to adopt a broadly activist ('I am because I act') or voluntarist ('I am because I choose') understanding of human nature which gave little place to indeterminacy, or what Keats calls 'negative capability'. So we have found ourselves in a position where theologically we have very few resources to rescue us from fundamentalist understandings of the fallenness of humanity, while philosphically we have given ourselves little alternative to a thoroughly activist view of the springs of human life. The result is that we believe ourselves to be either evil or in motion. Furthermore, when, under the influence of Freud and others, we have looked at the human 'inscape' we have found little to comfort us. This common view of ourselves as either fallen or in motion has been reinforced by a popular psychology which tells us that this condition is made worse by one or other of a number of incurable psychoses. Reason and the fall collude with a form of cheap Freudianism to give us no way out of our dilemma. What faults we have – and they are many – apparently have to be cured by activity. (Once again Dag Hammarskjöld's dictum comes to mind that in our day the road to holiness lies through the world of action.) If we cannot be good then the only remedy is to act good if we can, and even that is regarded as severely problematic. So, for modern men and women the human being is a despairing 'action man' driven to achieve an impossible goodness by will and reason. This is the prevailing self-understanding, but it is bleak in the extreme.

Thankfully, there have been signs within the past twenty or thirty years that this negative mind set will not prevail. There are indications that the postmodern condition will allow a return to the Church of a more positive anthropology, and one that does not underestimate the existence or the power of evil – evidence for which the twentieth century has seen enough. It should be said, of course, that the bleak landscape we have outlined has not been universal. There have always been those who have kept alive an alternative vision, but these have been in a minority – or at least they have been regarded as being a minority and certainly the Church, broadly speaking, has pandered to the ascendant point of view by assuming that it is somehow answerable to its negative critics. This sense of being entirely answerable to the rationalist critic has only fuelled the prevailing negativity and diminished the Church as a guardian of its own verities.

One of those who has gently refused to be overwhelmed by the prevailing voluntarist philosophy is Iris Murdoch. In her important book *The Sovereignty of Good*, Murdoch takes to task what she calls the prevailing 'existentialist view':

> I have classified together as existentialist both philosophers such as Sartre who claim the title, and philosophers such as Hampshire, Hare, Ayer, who do not. Characteristic of both is the identification of the true person with the empty, choosing will, and the corresponding emphasis upon the idea of movement rather than vision.[6]

She also says:

> I have used the word 'attention', which I borrow from Simone Weil, to express the idea of a just and living gaze directed upon an individual reality. I believe this to be the characteristic and proper mark of the active and moral agent.[7]

Murdoch believes that human beings deepen their moral appreciation and understanding of each other by *love and attention*. In actual fact we cannot avoid their influence, for in spite of our attempts to rule ourselves by reason and by will, love and attention are at work all the time anyway and will form us at a deep level. This is the cause of the sometimes very quirky behaviour of people in her novels. But if, instead of identifying ourselves with the willing, choosing, acting side of ourselves, we could realign ourselves with the *loving* and *attentive* side of our beings we would be more securely formed as human beings. Moral integrity comes from vision in the sense of what we really *see*. 'As moral agents we have to try to see justly, to overcome prejudice, to avoid temptation, to control and curb imagination, to direct reflection ... Man is not a combination of an impersonal, rational thinker and an impersonal will.' This means, of course, that a person is 'a unified being who sees and who desires in accord with what he sees'.[8]

Murdoch then moves on to explore the consequences of her approach for spirituality and concludes that 'Prayer is properly not petition but simply an attention to God which is a form of love'. This way of seeing is redemptive. It releases us from fantasy.

It is in the capacity to love, that is to see, that the liberation of the soul from fantasy consists. The freedom which is a proper human goal is the freedom from fantasy, that is the realism of compassion. What I have called fantasy, the proliferation of blinding self centred aims and images, is itself a powerful system of energy, and most of what is often called *will* or *willing* belongs to this system. What counteracts the system is attention to reality inspired by, consisting of, love. In the case of art and nature such attention is immediately rewarded by the enjoyment of beauty.[9]

What is important about Murdoch's understanding of the human person is that she does not react against a prevailing voluntarist point of view simply by returning to a static view of a human being as containing or constituted by an unchanging soul or self, what theologians would call an 'ontological' view. Her understanding is that human beings derive their freedom and their reality from their capacity to 'attend' and to see. This is a dynamic and relational view whereby human maturity is based upon an innate and necessary capacity to relate to what is *not* the self. This is a bridal anthropology where the human person is constituted by means of a marriage to the object of its seeking, a marriage to the object of our deepest attention, which, supremely speaking, is God.

While Iris Murdoch would have made no claims to be an orthodox believer, there are others who have enriched the contemporary Christian tradition by following in her wake, seeking to re-establish a contemporary anthropology of the human person within a Christian framework. Foremost among them, of course, is Hans Urs von Balthasar. As Iris Murdoch asked secular philosophy to move away from a voluntarist view, so von Balthasar asks Christian theology to move away from the action-based view of human selfhood to a more open-ended bridal anthropology whereby believers are constituted by the object of their contemplation. He takes the Danish theologian Søren Kierkegaard to task for eliminating the aesthetic from theology and insists that this makes far too sharp a distinction between agape – an active love – and eros – the love of desire – so robbing humanity of all joy. Such a criticism is important if only because it marks a shift in European theological thinking from commitment-based theologies to ones based upon attention to beauty or openness to the divine attraction. Much of twentieth-century theological thinking has, sometimes quite unconsciously, relied very heavily upon the former, and so upon Kierkegaard's criticism of aesthetics. Balthasar's move away from Kierkegaard is a significant development in European theology. He writes:

> Man is not merely addressed in a total mystery, as if he were compelled to accept obediently in blind and naked faith, something hidden from him, but that something is 'offered' to man by God, indeed offered in such a way that man can see it, understand it, make it his own, and live from it in keeping with his human nature.[10]

These words demonstrate that for von Balthasar human beings are constituted by their capacity to receive and respond to the approach of God. In an earlier work von Balthasar made this explicit when talking about the human capacity for contemplation:

> This gaze, this 'looking', is directed towards the perfect fulfilment promised to created nature in its entirety. In seeing and hearing God, it experiences the highest joy, that of being fulfilled in itself, but fulfilled by something infinitely greater than itself and, for that very reason, completely fulfilled and made blessed.[11]

The Cistercian monk and writer Thomas Merton makes these formal theological statements, more accessible in his meditations on the Promethean myth. Prometheus was, of course, the Greek hero who stole from the gods. Merton uses this myth on a number of occasions to illuminate the distinction between the common modern view that the individual can and indeed must conquer for him- or herself and the emphasis of the contemplative tradition which recognizes that the human condition is essentially one of a radical incompleteness which is fulfilled only by openness to the invisibility of God. This radical incompleteness allows the approach of the Bridegroom who, in the darkness of trust, comes to complete the Bride. Merton thus brings together a Christian understanding of the human heart as incomplete until completed by God with a rich understanding of the ongoing relevance of ancient mythology, in this case the story of Prometheus, combining them together to direct contemporary attention away from action-based myths of human completeness. This is a profoundly creative and powerful theological perception. Merton says:

One of the real reasons why Prometheus is condemned to be his own prisoner is because he is incapable of understanding the liberality of God. ... the fire he thinks he has to steal is after all his own fire. God created this spiritual fire for his own sons – more than that, He gives them His own uncreated and sanctifying fire which is the Holy Spirit. But Prometheus, who does not understand liberality since he has none of it in himself, refuses the gift of God.[12]

Merton of course, continues to develop this very un-Promethean view of human selfhood throughout his writing. But one of the keys to its understanding is to be found in the distinction he regularly makes between what he calls 'the false self' and 'the true self'. The false self is the product of our everyday sense of self, ambition and ego-centred living. It is that self which seeks to escape from the openness of living with God, which seeks to escape from the radical incompleteness of the self without God. The false self is that self which denies the bridal nature of the self and seeks to be the all-conquering Promethean hero. The false self is that self which seeks to live without the radical uncertainty of relatedness and all that this brings. In a striking metaphor Merton compares the false self to the dead Lazarus. When Lazarus emerges from the tomb in response to the summons of Christ he also emerges from the protection of the grave to face the uncertainty of God. The bandages around his hands and feet and over his face are, to Merton, the symbols of the captivity of the false self. Jesus commands that Lazarus be unloosed: 'Unbind him, and let him go.' The true self is hidden beneath the bandages we wind around the soul to protect it from the radical uncertainty with which it was born and which is the carrier of God. For the point about this true self is that it is not our possession. It is God's, or, more correctly, it is God abiding within us. Merton writes:

The true inner self, the true indestructible and immortal person, the true 'I' who answers to a new and secret name known only to himself and to God, does not 'have' anything, even 'contemplation'. This 'I' is not the kind of subject that can amass experiences, reflect on them, reflect on himself. ... This inmost self is beyond the kind of experience which says 'I want,' 'I love,' 'I know,' 'I feel.' It has its own way of knowing, loving and experiencing which is a divine way and not a human one, a way of

identity, of union, of 'espousal,' in which there is no longer a
separate psychological individuality drawing all good and truth
towards itself, and this loving and knowing for itself. Lover and
Beloved are 'one spirit'.[13]

This important passage reflects Merton's Cistercian heritage and the
bridal mysticism of St Bernard. It is significant because it reflects
upon that tradition in a modern context and uses it to speak to the
individualism and voluntarism of the present age.

It would be impossible, however, to leave this short review of the
re-emergence of a bridal mysticism in the twentieth century without
referring to the thinking of one or two of the so-called postmodernist
theologians who have taken centre stage in recent years. Whereas
postmodernist philosophy has not always been particularly sympathetic to the religious mentality, a certain amount of the writing of
this school has opened up ways of understanding the self which,
while setting the self free from the nineteenth- and early twentieth-
century verities, manage then to re-anchor the self in the mystery of
God. Two writers in particular are able to do this. The first is the
French theologian, René Girard.

Girard puts forward an anthropology of desire. He understands
human beings to be the products of what he calls 'mimetic' desire.
Our consciousness is formed by our desire to imitate others. He
believes that human beings are formed by their rivalry with others
and that societies, human groupings of all kinds, cohere because
people who are in rivalry with each other solve that rivalry by acting
together to evict the apparent cause of their rivalry from their midst.
There is a scapegoating mechanism at work in society by which
society evicts the 'unlike' in order to restore unity, especially when
that unity is threatened. Although this mimetic theory of human
behaviour appears deeply pessimistic, Girard posits 'a third
moment' (the first two moments being the moment of imitative
desire and the moment of unifying expulsion) when the perpetrators
of the scapegoating act realize something of what they have done
and come to think that there may be other means of securing human
unity. This he calls the moment of revealed discovery. It is one
which may well come about, Girard believes, through the impact
upon the human psyche of the revealed texts of scripture and the
telling and retelling of the story of Jesus, the one who accepted the
victimization inherent in his society. The moment of revealed

discovery occurs when the antique way of scapegoating as a means of preserving society and its unity is abandoned; but this 'moment' depends upon the prior or 'hidden' existence, in Girardian thinking, of a different anthropology.

In trying to come to terms with these new concepts it is important to remember that René Girard, along with other 'postmodern' thinkers, whether Christian or not, rejects the view of the self which much of contemporary western thinking inherits, namely that there is a 'self', an individual, isolatable human self, in each person which is the source of action and responsibility. This is the ontological view of the human person which, the postmodernist believes, lies behind so many of our contemporary ills. What characterizes the postmodern thinker is his or her view that such a self does not exist, but is in fact a construct, something we have invented in order to preserve the social status quo. Clearly, for those postmodern thinkers who have no allegiance to the Christian tradition, such a view leads to a form of nihilism or relativism about the self; but not so for René Girard. Girard's analysis moves postmodernism beyond nihilism. What he suggests is that human beings are formed by the relationships of desire between ourselves. What I want and what others want of me is what makes me. But a moment's thought will show that this implies that human beings are inevitably locked into a degree of conflict, and that violence cannot be avoided. Let James Alison, Girard's most influential interpreter in the English-speaking theological world, explain this:

> In this way, we can say that every human being is, in fact, constituted by and with an in-built relationality to the other which formed him or her. This other constituted the very possibility of human desire. We can also say that owing to the way in which we are in fact constituted, that desire is rivalistic and builds identity, to a greater or lesser extent, by denial of the alterity, and the anteriority, of the other desire. That is to say, human desire, as we know it, works by grasping and appropriating being rather than receiving it. In this sense we are always already locked into the other which forms us in a relationship of acquisitive mimesis, that is, in a relationship of violence which springs from, and leads to, death.[14]

Girard further argues that we become conscious that this is how human beings work because something new and different has occurred, that is, the arrival in human form of a being who was not locked into these deathly sequences of imitative desire. This is the one human being who was made historically present as a self-giving and forgiving victim. The presence of this other, within the historical process, sets us free to see what has been going on and releases us from the processes which we thought had formed us and which we thought were inevitable. Because of Jesus and his capacity to live completely within the freedom of God, human beings discover that they too can live simply and gratuitously, in total freedom. James Alison explains:

> We have, then, in any given human being, a self formed by the desire of another. That desire is lived in rivalistic inflection, what I have called desire of grasping or appropriation. We also have the discovery that the possibility of the existence of any desire at all was an anterior desire that is in no sense rivalistic, which we call the creative love of God. The gratuity of God's love works precisely and only as self-giving; working to produce in each human a capacity to accept – as purely gratuitous – the self-giving other. ... The great anthropological transformation, therefore, is of the way in which we move from being constituted by an anterior desire which moves us into deadlock, by grasping and appropriating our sense of being, to being constituted by a self-giving other that can be received only as constantly and per-petually self-giving, as gratuitous, and therefore never grasped, never appropriated, but only received and shared.[15]

Girard's anthropology thus appears to bow towards the nihilism of the present age by recognizing the apparent inevitability of rivalry and the violence it engenders, but it is only a temporary bow. For he then shows that the very desire which locks the modern world into conflict can be the same desire which frees it once this desire discovers that it can be subverted from within by the presence of a self-giving other made known in history in the work and teaching of Jesus, the self-giving and forgiving victim. So Bernard's bridal anthropology comes into its own in a clearly postmodern context. René Girard confirms in modern terms the ancient perception of the Cistercian tradition that human beings are constituted by the arrival of the self-giving Bridegroom to whom they must, if they wish to be anything at all, open themselves and then receive and share who he is.

Girard looks at the self in the context of salvation and the human need to be saved from an inherent violence. Another postmodern theologian discovers, or rediscovers, the centrality of the bridal anthropology of which we have been speaking in the context of his study of the doctrine of the Trinity. The traditional trinitarian affirmation of 'three persons in one God' presents the modern mind with a number of problems, the most immediate being that the statement appears to affirm a form of threeness in God, a tritheism, for to most modern minds 'person' implies a substantive individual. Much of this difficulty, however, derives from the modern preoccupation with individuality and the importance of 'personality' as a defining characteristic of what is human. Once that is ignored or abandoned then it becomes possible to rediscover the importance and centrality of the doctrine of the Trinity. This is because what the traditional word 'persons' in the phrase 'three persons in one God' indicates is not, by and large, what the contemporary mind understands by 'persons'. The 'persons' of the Trinity are not persons in the modern sense. As David Cunningham says:

> There is nothing sacred about the term *person*; even Augustine admitted that he finally chose the Latin word persona only in order not to be reduced to silence when asked 'Three whats?' One answer might be 'three relations'; Augustine himself develops this notion at length.[16]

So, it might be said, did Thomas Aquinas:

> I think it will be clear that Aquinas's doctrine gives us no warrant for saying that there are three persons in God; for 'person' in English undoubtedly means an individual subject, a distinct centre of consciousness. Now the consciousness of the Son is the consciousness of the Father and of the Holy Spirit, it is simply God's consciousness. There are not three knowledges or three lovings in God. The Word is simply the way in which God is self-conscious, knows what he is, as the Spirit simply is the delight God takes in what he is when he is knowing it. If we say that there are three persons in God, in the ordinary sense of person, we are tritheists.[17]

Building on that understanding, David Cunningham elaborates a way of looking at the Trinity which requires a relational view of the persons within the Trinity and, also, a relational view of the human self which is then able to participate in the divine life of the trinitarian God. He looks for support in this to the postmodern philosophers of the self and remarks how the last few decades have witnessed 'a declining confidence in the portrait of human subjectivity that was developed in the Enlightenment – the notion of an autonomous self, capable of exercising its freedom in supreme isolation from the rest of the world. The subject has been "de-centred".'[18]

What Cunningham avers is that such a 'de-centring' is actually a discovery, a gain rather than, as it might be assumed, a loss, because it is precisely what happens in God. The doctrine of the Trinity is a way of talking about God by which she is 'de-centred' and becomes relational. This is also precisely what is the case with human beings. We are not isolated subjects, but persons who are only so in relationship with others, only ourselves when 'visited' by others. The point is that we have allowed an Enlightenment preoccupation with the supreme and isolated choosing self to obscure not just the reality of who we are, but also the reality of God. When we understand ourselves in this sense we will not only have a happier and more healthy view of ourselves but we will also be able to return to a faith in the trinitarian God who is God in relationship.

Cunningham elaborates a postmodern view of the self-in-relation, what he calls *participation*.

> This continuous process of the composition, decomposition, and recomposition of the self is what I am trying to invoke with the category of *participation*. We are not isolated entities; we exist as 'persons' only insofar as we participate in others, and they in us, to such a degree that the construal of the 'self' is constantly being broken down, and reconstituted anew, in the intimacy of this mutual participation.[19]

This radical openness of the self to the other, indeed the assertion that the self does not exist except in radical openness to the other is, in principle, a rediscovery of the bridal anthropology of the Cistercian world; but not only that, it is also a rediscovery which allows belief in, and participation in the trinitarian God of Christian tradition to become possible once again. Cunningham's restatement of the self in postmodern terms is also a restatement of the doctrine of the Trinity as traditionally held but latterly lost because we were seeing both the self and God through the spectacles of Enlightenment thinking.

So we need a different view of the self if we are to do theology properly in the twenty-first century. We need a view of the self which is not dominated by reason, will and action, but one which is happy to live with loving attention, one which is content to live with an openness to whatever God offers, one which is content to live with what has been already given rather than striving, like Prometheus, to steal fire from the gods. The modern emphasis on rationality, choice and action, and the elevation of these aspects of human nature to be determinative or supreme, have left human beings bereft, rudderless, open to the most severe onslaughts upon the soul because nothing forms them. While it is true that human beings – or at least those human beings that live in the economically developed parts of the world – live longer and with enormous degrees of comfort, it is also true that they are subject to violence as never before and live a deeply divided and alienated life. The beginning of the recovery of wholeness and peace is rooted in the rediscovery of the incompleteness of the self, the re-enchantment of the self by the announcement that the Bridegroom cometh. If we can bear to live with this sort of self then we will be agents of moral integrity, people of prayer and people of loving attention to God and others. Moreover, we will lead what I would call the contemplative or the monastic, or properly speaking, the mystical life.

It is well known that St Bernard insisted on simplicity in the architecture of Cistercian churches. It is true that this simplicity was an attempt to reassert the original Benedictine simplicity over against the excesses of Cluny and Abbot Sugar. But there is a more profound and perhaps unconscious reason for their simplicity. Church space mirrors the space within the human person. Elaboration distracts and undermines the essential readiness required of the attentive soul for the arrival of the Bridegroom. The simplicity of the Cistercian liturgical space is a constant reminder of the necessity for the human person to remain open and ready. The Cistercian church is a statement in stone of the Cistercian understanding of the soul, one in which the lamps trimmed in readiness for the Bridegroom.

5
'I will give you a voice'
The Re-enchantment
of Speech

The American writer Annie Dillard has an essay which she calls *Teaching a Stone to Talk*.[1] In it she describes a strange man she once knew who lived on an island off the west coast of America and who kept a stone on his mantelpiece. For some reason it was normally kept covered by a piece of coloured leather, but every morning he would uncover it and give it lessons in talking, as if it were a parrot or a child. At first we find this very strange and are tempted to dismiss the essay and put the book away. But if we read on we are illuminated, for Annie Dillard points out that the silence of nature is our self-inflicted destiny. This is what we have wished upon ourselves. We have in fact decided that the creation is silent, that it is 'not holy', and we live where we want to live because we want to do the talking.

She also points out that we have been faced with the silence of the universe not simply since the Enlightenment – which is where many contemporary theological writers would place the beginnings of our present condition – but since our wandering in the desert at Sinai. This is the mythical origin of our present condition. It lies deeper than we had imagined and so cannot be retrieved simply by attempting to reverse the effects of the Enlightenment upon our culture. There is more to it than that. For there, in the desert, we heard God speaking and found it far too loud. The record is clear. 'All the people saw the thunderings, and the lightnings, and the noise of the trumpet, and the mountain smoking.'[2] And it scared them witless. And they said to Moses, it's all right, *you* can speak to us, but please, never let God speak to us: 'Do not let God speak to us, or we will die.'

And what we have asked for is what we have been given. For the record shows that God agreed to our request and sent us back to our tents and to a silence that ever since we have found unbearable, and to a darkness that we have not been able to cope with. The consequence is that we have filled the darkness with artificial light of our own making and the silence with words which we have invented. But there is a form of torture in this condition, a sense of *anomie*, hence the strange actions of the young man who attempts to reverse the silence of nature by teaching a stone to talk. But it is not just his torture, it is also our own. It is the condition of the western man or woman. We have all poured water over the burning bush and do not know how to rekindle it. We have all blown away the smoke and the fire and are left wondering why all that remains in our mouths is the taste of ashes. All our modernism has left us with is the 'microphoned voice' spoken of by the theologians we referred to earlier.

Every now and then we do break through this silence and we receive glimpses into a reality which has been hidden from us since our wanderings in the desert. We glimpse that the universe is not silent but full of noises. Science occasionally penetrates the silence of the cosmos to discover noises that it cannot interpret: the song of the whales who communicate with each other at vast distances and by means of 'tunes' or 'sound bites' that we cannot 'hear' but which change month by month and pod by pod; the noise of the stars, both those coming into being and those dying; other 'noises' which we know are there but which we cannot receive. And then, perchance, we might read Psalm 65 and find that there is a speech there after all, a speech that the psalmists knew about all along; there is a speech in creation, for the valleys shout and sing together for joy.

There is, of course, a difference between post-Enlightenment thinking about nature, thinking which regards nature as neutral or dead, and pre-Enlightenment thinking, when the universe was naturally understood to be alive with the praise of God; but the difference is greater than the historical distinction. Behind the historical distinction there lies a more profound existential distinction, a faith distinction between the readiness to hear the speech of creation and to participate in it and the refusal to hear and participate. The rise of and the existence of the Enlightenment in the eighteenth and nineteenth centuries in one sense only symbolizes this deeper existential division. Contemporary criticism of our over-reliance upon Enlightenment thinking would, properly speaking, be more acceptable if it was also aware of that deeper existential division between readiness and the potentially inhuman refusal to hear the speech of the creation.

The Fathers of the early Church were aware of the speech of creation and spoke of it in terms of prayer. They took the view that the whole creation prayed, and there are some remarkable passages in the writings of the early Church which illustrate this. There is, for example, a lovely passage in *The Apostolic Tradition* which encourages us to pray during the night as monks did and still do: 'We have to pray at this hour because all creation rests for a moment in order to praise the Lord. The stars, the trees, the rivers stop for an instant and together with the choir of angels and the souls of the righteous, sing the praises of God.'[3]

The Fathers take the words of St Paul seriously, where he speaks of the whole creation 'groaning and travailing together', and interpret this as the groaning of prayer and the sighing of creation for its maker and redeemer. The prayer of longing is the essential speech of all created things. Gregory of Nazianzus puts this clearly in one of his *Dogmatic Poems*:

All creatures praise thee,
those that speak and those that are dumb.
All creatures bow down before thee,
Those that can think and those that have no power of thought.
The universal longing, the groaning of creation tends towards thee.
Everything that exists prays to thee
And to thee every creature that can read thy universe
Sends up a hymn of silence.[4]

When we pray we should understand, then, that we are participating in the primary speech of creation, we are returning to hearing and responding to the speech of God. The original insight of the Fathers, which we have lost, is that prayer is the original, natural and uninhibited speech of the creation, ourselves included, in praise of God. That prayer is what we were made for. This is an insight which turns on its head the modern assumption that prayer is something which you have to learn, as if it were essentially something unnatural or alien to humanity which can well do without such things. Once this point is understood then we shall begin to see prayer as not being our own speech, not something which it is ours to create, but rather as the work of the Spirit, God's speech within us, the speech in which we participate by grace and faithfulness, but which we have lost touch with. The phrase 'primary speech' has been used by two writers on prayer who say in their own way what Gregory of Nazianzus was saying in his. They say, 'Prayer is that primordial discourse in which we assert, however clumsily or eloquently, our own being.'[5]

And, of course, the insight of the earlier tradition was that prayer is a participation in the language of the Trinity, for the converse between the Father, the Son and the Holy Spirit is that which makes all things and in which all prayer participates. Origen says in his treatise *On Prayer*:

> Anyone who prays shares in the prayer of the Word of God, who is present among those who do not know him and is not absent from anyone's prayer. The Son prays to the Father in union with the believer whose mediator he is. The Son of God is, in fact, the high priest of our offerings and our advocate with the Father. He prays for those who pray and pleads with those who plead.[6]

To pray, then, is to recover our lost speech and to dare once more to allow God to speak to us and, indeed, within us. In reality, this is what is always happening in creation and it is this in which humanity is called to participate. This insight, although lost to many rationally minded Christians, has not been lost to poets and writers. The Irish poet Seamus Heaney speaks of it. In commenting on the work of the Russian dissident poet Osip Mandelstam, he remarks how Mandelstam's wife Nadezhda described her husband's work on a poem as 'a dig for the nugget of harmony' and said that 'the search for lost words is an attempt to remember what is still to be brought into being'. Heaney then develops this theme of poetry being the search for lost words when he writes about the work of Elizabeth Bishop, the twentieth-century American poet who would spend months in the crafting of each of her poems. In talking about her poem *At the Fishhouses*, Heaney says:

> The concluding lines ... possess that *sine qua non* of all lyric utterance, a completely persuasive inner cadence which is deeply intimate with the laden water of full tide. The lines are inhabited by certain profoundly true tones, which as Robert Frost put it, 'were before words were, living in the cave of the mouth', and they do what poetry most essentially does: they fortify our

inclination to credit promptings of our intuitive being. They help us to say in the first recesses of ourselves, in the shyest, pre-social part of our nature, 'Yes, I know something like that too. Yes, that's right; thank you for putting words on it.'[7]

So the poet knows something of the search for the lost words of God within us and helps to retrieve them from 'the cave of the mouth'.

But it is not just the Catholic poet who comes to the conclusion that there are 'words which were before words were', it is also the Jewish biblical scholar. Carol Ochs, in her important study of the relationship between biblical spirituality and human holiness, remarks that in the Hebrew scriptures sound has primacy over sight. She traces, through the historic narrative, the struggle between the priestly tradition which emphasizes 'seeing' and 'glory' and the prophetic tradition which, she says, eventually triumphs, and which emphasizes 'hearing' and 'the word'. She writes:

> When sound takes priority, salvation is not undertaken individu-ally to achieve personal bliss, it is pursued by those who can hear, for the sake of all others. Western thought depicts enlightenment as coming from darkness to light ... the Bible emphasizes an oral rather than a visual tradition. Where the Western philosopher fears darkness, the biblical thinker fears silence ... Our own silence is not fearsome – it is essential, so that the voice of God can be heard.[8]

These words immediately remind us of the account of the encounter with God at Sinai as understood by Annie Dillard, who implies that the people of Israel, symbolizing all of us, wanted to speak with God but found that he spoke too loudly for them to bear it, so in their fear they endured the silence they did not want. Carol Ochs goes on to suggest that the original speech of God was in reality a song which creates and which continues to sing within creation. It is this song, she says, that we need to hear for our own forgiveness, wholeness and redemption. She reminds us of the words of T. S. Eliot:

> ... music heard so deeply
> That it is not heard at all, but you are the music
> While the music lasts.[9]

Our inability to hear real speech, the word of God, is the ultimate problem. We make ourselves deaf with the sound of our own words and so fail to hear the original mystical speech of God who is too real, too frightening for us to face. The consequence is that we are reduced to a narrow human language of our own and it is this language that we use to speak about God when in reality we should either use no language at all, sending up, as Gregory says, a hymn of silence, listening for the divine word in the darkness of ourselves and allowing that word to speak within us; or, perhaps, we should use every linguistic device known to us in order to echo something of the divine music which flows through the whole creation. It seems that neither is possible.

Neither is possible to us because we live in an age when our capacity for speech is vastly reduced. It is not possible for us to hear the original speech of God or to allow that speech to utter itself within us. And so we cannot pray as we were created to pray, and follow the mystical way, while we are unconvinced or unaware that there is any speech beyond our own. While we believe that language and speech is ours, we shall be continually reduced to the 'Newspeak' of George Orwell's novel *1984*, or, to quote a more recent parallel, we shall be reduced to what the poet Les Murray, in perhaps an unconscious echo of Orwell's term, calls 'Narrowspeak'. No progress will be made by the Church or by Christians in the mystical way until they come to realize that there is a further speech which utters them and which is the speech of God, what Les Murray calls 'Wholespeak'.

It would be helpful to look at what Murray says, for he too is convinced of the need to re-enchant the Christian mind and so to release us into the mystical awareness which we so sadly lack in the twenty-first century. Murray is an Australian poet and a practising Catholic. In 1986 he was asked to deliver the Aquinas Lecture, which he called 'Embodiment and Incarnation'. In it he begins by talking about the making of anthologies of poetry, two of which he has just completed. He found that not everybody had understood what he was trying to do in such anthologies except an Anglican poet who said that the anthology in question worked on the basis that the poet and the theologian covered much the same ground. Murray agrees and, quoting Thomas Aquinas, goes on to say that the poetic experience, somewhat like religion, is a radiant one but one which we cannot tolerate all of the time. We have to find a way of expressing the radiance. We do after all have two modes of consciousness, waking and dreaming, and we must keep these in harmony. But just as we need to dream, so we need to speak about our dreams in words which can contain them. He then makes the powerful suggestion that all of the systems, ideologies, religions and other loyalties by which we live our lives are in fact fusions of the waking and the dreaming state, they are 'poems' which combine and attempt to balance vision and reasoning. He says:

> I may find, say, the poem of science too cerebral and too poorly integrated on its dream side ... but for some it serves as the poem of their lives, and they may find Catholicism, as they understand it, to be aberrant to reason in some way, or distorted in what the Germans might call its dreamwork, lacking warrant from the unconscious for some of its claims.[10]

All of this is quite fascinating and somewhat unexplored in British theological circles. Very few contemporary theologians, if any at all,[11] have dared to suggest that the Enlightenment project – what Murray calls 'the science poem' – is in itself a metaphor put together by human beings in order to make sense of our existence here. Most are still battling with the Enlightenment project as if it were absolute truth and are still trying to find ways and means of reconciling religion with science, as if neither science nor religion were by any stretch of the imagination 'poems' or metaphors. No wonder we have lost our capacity to speak of or to entertain the mystical in our lives.

Murray then introduces the two crucial terms which elucidate his thinking even further – Narrowspeak and Wholespeak. In an important paragraph he says:

> I call properly integrated poetic discourse Wholespeak, while discourses based on the supposed primacy or indeed exclusive sovereignty of daylight reason I call Narrowspeak. The former embraces all good poetry including that of religion, the latter embraces most of the administrative discourse by which the world is ruled from day to day, as well as most of criticism. ... We have come, over the last few centuries to think that we live in a prose universe, with prose as the norm of all discourse. This is a cause, or a consequence, of the decline in belief in creation (*poesis*). In fact, descriptive prose doesn't answer to our own inner nature, and so cannot describe the cosmos adequately.[12]

Murray says that the majority of verse published in literary journals is written in Narrowspeak and certainly evinces 'interest', or appeals to excitement or innovation or relevance, but this is only to show how it is really the product of a spiritually starved period, since real poetry 'has its own authority and needs make no such appeals'. This is important since it enables us to see clearly not just what has happened to poetry, Murray's immediate concern, but also what has happened to theology in general and mystical theology in particular.

On the whole in our day we have come to the view within the churches that talk about God has to be conducted in language which everybody can understand and which appeals to relevance or excitement or innovation. Inevitably, therefore, most theology of any consequence, and the large parts of our liturgies, are written in prose because, as Murray says, we think that this is a prose universe and that prose is the normal and natural form of discourse. Prose, we believe, is what communicates. We have come to believe that is all we have, or at least all we need. We have become content, or have convinced ourselves, that anything else will lead to obfuscation, and so we talk about God or we talk to God almost entirely in Narrowspeak. It seems that we do not believe that we can have any real access to Wholespeak, for that is the language either of God alone or maybe of demons and so must be carefully avoided. In any case God is silent; God no longer speaks to us directly; we have to speak about him or to him in our own language. This is a truly tragic situation, because a Church which speaks entirely in Narrowspeak cannot answer to the ultimate longings of the human person, nor can it indeed, and more centrally, speak to the human world properly of God. Above all, such a Church is one which appears to believe that God has stopped talking. This is because those longings and those words from God to us are only really best expressed in Wholespeak, a language which is, as Murray says, 'truly dreamed'. At the end of the essay Murray talks about Jesus who 'lives on the level of poetry ... He never speaks in abstractions; there seems to be no Narrowspeak in him.' Jesus speaks of the Kingdom but, 'The Kingdom is Jesus' own poem, and he embodies it fully.' Jesus becomes the word of God which we have been awaiting since the silence of God was announced on Sinai. He it is who embodies the Kingdom, who is the poem of which he speaks, in whom is no Narrowspeak at all.

Murray's essay shows that we are left with two possibilities. Either we remain with the silence of God, giving ourselves no other possibilities than Narrowspeak, the prose of our own making, since God is other than ourselves and does not speak to us at all. Or else we allow ourselves the possibility of poetry, of Wholespeak, of allowing the beauty and the terror and the fear portrayed in Sinai to become real once again in the face of Jesus, and allow ourselves to hear the speech of God once again. Once we do that, once we allow ourselves to become faithful, then we have no alternative but to follow the patterns of Wholespeak and to allow the word to be spoken within us.

This is the beginning of the mystical way and the way which the Church, when faithful, has constantly and consistently trod. It is the mystical way simply because once we allow God to be the speaker then we can no longer consider her to be the object of our speech; she is then no longer an object at all since she is the source of that which speaks us. Once we remove God from the realm of object, once we say that the language which is spoken in the Church, indeed in life, is not ours, does not have its source in us, then we cannot be the objective knowers or the speakers who speak about God as if she were somebody or something which could be described or seen by us. He it is who speaks, and our being, our speech, is but part of his. We are spoken, indeed we are seen, breathed, dreamed by God who is the source of all making. She is 'the Maker of al thing', including us and including our speech. Once we come to understand that God is not the subject of our speech or our seeing, indeed cannot be the subject of anything of that kind without abandoning being God, then there is a real sense in which we cannot know anything about him, at least in the sense of knowing and possessing that which we know. We can only be known by she who is the maker, the speaker of the word of making. This has an immediate and overwhelming consequence for the manner of our speaking about God and our speaking to God. Our theology has to derive from being known. It cannot be the result of our human knowing. We are those who know only that we are known and only speak that which we are given to speak.

What is being said here is that language – in particular theological language, but ultimately all language – is derived from the fact that we are known by God and his knowing of us makes our speech possible. Speech which is our own, or which claims to be our own, is inadequate and, ultimately, without meaning. This means that in order to release true meaning in our speech it has to derive from our capacity to address our speech to God, not simply in terms of intellectual discourse, for God is not simply another human intelligence that we can speak to, but in terms which make sense of the relationship between the creator and the created, namely praise. All truly meaningful speech is, properly speaking, derived from an act or attitude of praise and is therefore essentially doxological in character.

The German poet Rilke, towards the end of his great struggle to produce his best work, wrote a series of sonnets for Orpheus. The seventh sonnet reads:

> Praising that's it! As a praiser and blesser
> he came like the ore from the taciturn mine.
> Came with his heart, Oh transient presser,
> for men, of a never-exhaustible wine.[13]

It is worth remembering that this is the most extraordinary development – for Rilke was born into a very repressive, suffocating bourgeois family. His mother had longed for a daughter and in his childhood used to dress Rilke as a girl and call him Sophie. His relations with women were by turns passionate and withdrawn. He struggled all his life with the legacy of this bourgeois upbringing. But his final poetry (the *Duino Elegies* and the *Sonnets to Orpheus*) is magnificent. After a long struggle he produces verse which is full of triumph; of protest, yes, but of triumph against shallowness, of seeing things merely as things. The poet is the one who, by his capacity for attention, wrests from objects their inner intensity and depth.

> For when the traveler returns from the mountain-slopes into the
>   valley,
> he brings, not a handful of earth, unsayable to others, but instead
> some word he had gained, some pure word, the yellow and blue
> gentian. Perhaps we are *here* in order to say: house,
> bridge, fountain, gate, pitcher, fruit-tree, window ... But to *say*
>   them, you must understand,
> oh, to say them *more* intensely than the Things themselves
> ever dreamed of existing...[14]

And later he wrote:

> one earthly thing, truly experienced, even once, is enough for a
>   lifetime...
> Truly, being here is glorious...[15]

Rilke is not the only poet to have come to this conclusion. But Rilke comes to the central conclusion that praise, or praising, is what we are here for; it is what makes sense of how we are to be, and the object of praise is quite simply all that is; we have to find the simple, pure words, 'house, bridge, fountain'. Rilke, of course, was not an orthodox Christian and had a great deal of criticism of the Church and orthodox Catholicism – perhaps because his suffocating mother had been such a rigorous Catholic – but his insight about the primary function of human existence and so the primary function of language is an insight which is only now being incorporated into the mainstream of theological writing.

It is an insight which is shared by a number of the contemporary theologians we have already met who bear the epithet 'postmodern'. One of the most influential of these is Catherine Pickstock. In her book *After Writing*,[16] she puts forward a thesis about how we have come to use language in the European tradition. She suggests that this tradition has witnessed a battle over the nature of language from the time of Plato. Plato's arguments were, she says, for an understanding of language as primarily doxological, existing for, and only receiving meaning when used ultimately for, the praise of the divine. Language is ultimately liturgical and human beings therefore ultimately liturgical beings. She argues that there was a battle between Plato and the Sophists of his day on this point, in which Plato triumphed, and that the early and medieval Church used language in the Platonic manner, that is, as doxological – for the praise of the divine. There was, however, another battle towards the end of the Middle Ages when the doxological use of language was reduced and sidelined by the influence of a number of philosophers – Duns Scotus and William of Occam in particular – who, in the end, had an enormous influence on the reformers. Language then lost its primarily doxological or open-ended 'enchanted' qualities and was used in a different way. Pickstock calls this process of the diminution or reduction of the doxological quality of language 'spatialization'. It is a process in which language comes to refer only to things, it is used 'spatially'. She says this process began at the end of the medieval period but was finally confirmed by Descartes and then the Enlightenment. We now live with the results of the death of language as liturgical and doxological and live in an enclosed world with little or no capacity to use language in a way which enables it to refer *out* of itself. Language is totally determined by the observable world. Spatialization and, importantly, 'capital' then triumph.

Catherine Pickstock suggests that we do now have a window of opportunity in which to put things right. The emergence of the inadequacy of the modern, its inability to deliver the peaceful and secure world which it promised, is an opportunity rather than a disaster. The postmodern situation is, in fact, a gift to the Church, releasing the Church to be Church and to develop its own language once again. We are no longer obliged to adopt the language of modernity in which to speak to the modern world. Catherine Pickstock takes this challenge seriously in several essays which take to task the modern liturgical tendency to speak in apparently plain, modern language, arguing that this obscures rather than releases the divine. She urges the way of re-enchantment. We can rebuild the liturgical city. We can re-enchant the Church instead of simply adapting the language of the wider culture or using the language of this culture in the liturgy.

Pickstock takes up themes which are essential to the reconstructive theological work of another theologian, John Milbank. Milbank seeks 'to develop a specifically theological account of language' and wishes to show 'how a theology which takes "language" as one of its central preoccupations, but language construed in a specifically theological manner, might treat its traditional themes of God and Creation, God the Son, the Incarnation, the Holy Spirit, Christian life and Christian society'.[17]

For both Pickstock and Milbank, approaches to theology which seek for the foundations of theology apart from or prior to its meditation in and through language are impossible. This is because 'we can never step outside of the network of sign-making' and the real itself is linguistic, and 'the human being is a linguistic being which participates in the divine linguistic being'.[18] Central to John Milbank's understanding is the view that nothing exists outside of the language of God and that our own language is but a participation in that divine speaking. So once again the contemporary 'postmodern' theologians illuminate both the deathly quality of modern speech, described by Les Murray as 'Narrow-speak', and urge us to see the whole of creation as 'spoken', and so our own speech as part of that original spokenness. What our own speech is not and cannot be reduced to is plain speech about some other reality. It is itself part of the enchanted reality which is part of the spokenness of God.

Let me conclude with some important words by George Steiner.

＊ p.193 Seasons of the Spirit quoting Murray 'Poet as Theologian'

We flinch from the immediate pressures of mystery in poetic, in aesthetic acts of creation as we do from the realization of our diminished humanity, of all that is literally bestial in the murderousness and gadgetry of this age. The secondary is our narcotic. Like sleepwalkers, we are guarded by the numbing drone of the journalistic, of the theoretical, from the often harsh, imperious radiance of sheer presence. Beauty can, indeed, be 'terribly born', as Yeats says. The cry of those Angels in Rilke's Duino Elegies can embarrass intolerably. The news brought by annunciations not only stays new; it can be unendurable in its ambiguity. So we slide past the singing rocks, their song stifled or made artifice, by secular gloss and critique.

I sense that we shall not come home to the facts of our unhousedness, of our eviction from a central humanity in the face of the tidal provocations of political barbarism and technocratic servitude, if we do not redefine, if we do not re-experience, the life of meaning in the text, in music, in art. We must come to recognize, and the stress is on re-cognition, a meaningfulness which is that of a freedom of giving and of reception beyond the constraints of immanence.[19]

6
'But dwelt at home ...'
The Re-enchantment
of Action

Two incidents from my ministry will illuminate what I want to say.
The first is not unique and could be repeated by most pastors. In one
of my parishes lived an insurance surveyor who travelled the South
West of England advising large companies to insure their units,
whether they were mines or factories or whatever. He was an
extremely busy man, driving hundreds of miles every week. And he
rang me one day and said he wanted to talk, so we agreed to meet for
lunch. I thought in my professional way that he had a problem that
he wanted to talk to me about. Not a bit of it – he thought *I* had a
problem. As we sat sipping our beer he said, 'Your trouble is that
you're getting to be like me – far too busy. Somehow you must slow
down. You ought to be in the position where, if I or somebody like
me rings up in a crisis, you can offer me any one of two evenings in
that week.' Any parish priest knows how impossible that is. Of
course, I laughed, but he was serious and had a point about the
lifestyle of the parson or, in one sense, about the lifestyle of any of
us.

The second story concerns somebody who for some time came to
me for spiritual advice. She is a psychotherapist and for a long time
she was in therapy. As part of her training she was required to write
a dissertation in partial fulfilment of the requirements to qualify in
her chosen profession. She chose to write about the relationship
between psychotherapy and spirituality. Part of the dissertation was
a considered reflection on her experiences in therapy. She was
fortunate in her choice of therapist who was a Jungian-inclined

practitioner who was able to provide the environment in which my
friend was able to begin to reconnect with her true self:

> My experience of this period of my therapy was of lying for long
> periods in depressed silence and inarticulate silence during which
> I experienced my therapist as providing a holding and containing
> presence communicated to me not through interpretative inter-
> ventions but by allowing herself to be felt and heard by me in the
> different rhythms of her breathing and the movement of her body
> conveyed through the creaking of her chair.[1]

In other words, there was a form of sympathetic silence between
them. She goes on to say:

> It was towards the end of my long, depressed silence in therapy that
> the surprising thought and desire came that I wanted to seek sacra-
> mental confession – the wish arising not from neurotic guilt but a
> recognition that what had happened should not have happened. It
> was the beginning of a reconciliation with a faith from which I had
> become traumatically estranged – a reconciliation that led to the
> development of a contemplative capacity, the reawakening of a
> sense of inner aliveness and a capacity to symbolize. It is in this re-
> connection with a sense of true self that I understand as enabling a
> capacity to be alone by which I mean not solely actual physical
> solitude but rather a capacity to become truly comfortable with the
> experience of 'I am who I am' then this experience is one of the
> distinguishing experiences of a contemplative capacity. Contem-
> plation, said Thomas Aquinas, is the simple enjoyment of the truth.

She rediscovered, through the contemplative presence of her
therapist, a contemplative capacity within herself which returned
her to holy Church. She made her confession and she is now fully
re-established within the Church and being considered for the
priesthood. She had rediscovered the contemplative or mystical way.

A capacity to be a contemplative presence is what my overworked
insurance surveyor needed, what my psychotherapist friend needed
and discovered, and it is precisely this that much of the current
pastoral practice of the Church, with its emphasis on mission,
management and marketing, finds it difficult to represent. What I
believe we need is a strategy for the recovery of the contemplative
pastor. The Church needs pastors and people who are aware of the
reality represented by Thomas Aquinas' statement that contempla-

tion is the simple enjoyment of the truth, knowing that the truth of which he speaks is the truth about ourselves as much as the truth about the universe. I believe this recovery is possible within the mass of competing forces within the life of the Church provided that we hold a number of things in mind. Our priorities must be re-ordered.

The first priority in any programme for the recovery of the contemplative or 'mystical' Christian is for all of us to live out a refusal of definitions and roles. In one country parish I was known to many of the older people as 'Parson' and they would say 'Parson said' or whatever. They wouldn't refer to me as 'Vicar' or even by my name, quite simply as 'Parson'. After an initial surprise I came to appreciate this term because it was a term which defied definition. It comes, of course, from the Middle English word for person and its use indicates what each member of the clergy should be, a representative person. Everybody else in the parish was apparently defined by their role – he or she was an accountant, a butcher, a schoolteacher, a housewife – but I was nothing. I was the one without any specific, professional role because I was quite simply the person in that place. And in one sense the priest represents what the whole community of the Church should be, that it should be persons. The problem is that the culture of the day finds persons without roles or definitions quite difficult to accept and understand.

This is particularly appropriate for the parish priest and as such is well picked up by a writer on the nature of pastoral ministry. Christopher Moody, in his book *Eccentric Ministry*, says that in the ministry of a priest those encounters with other people which are by their nature fleeting and obscure are undervalued and neglected in favour of those over which we have most control. This is the result of over-professional development and it restricts pastoral activity to a narrower and narrower field in a society where more and more contacts are actually of a transitory nature. He believes it important for pastors 'to ask what might be gained by trying to work in the full knowledge that we are not entirely in control, either of the situations to which we are introduced, or of what we are held to represent by the other participants'.[2] Moody then goes on to relate an incident which occurred when he was chaplain to a large city college and the college began to develop a more professional structure for student services, including pastoral care, and he was forced to think through his role in the institution. Interestingly he found himself wanting to serve the institution in a way which did not lock him in to the role of a professional in pastoral care, even if this care was seen to be somehow spiritually based. He says:

> In the course of thinking things through I did indeed come to feel that my understanding of the pastoral task had become too detached from its roots in the belief that God is dynamically at work, immanently and redemptively, in his own creation towards a final fulfilment. It is our privilege as pastors ... to discern this activity in whatever situation we are called and, in some way, to release and embody it in our own lives. To return to these roots means, I believe, to discard many of the notions about professional pastoral ministry which have helped to imprison this activity within church congregations, and to reach back to a different understanding of it.[3]

It is interesting and important that somebody as involved as the author of these words in the active and busy ministry of a city parish and a city college should feel that the best way of embodying pastoral care was 'to reach back' to an earlier understanding of how pastoral care is to be done which did not involve definitions and roles but specifically avoided them.

This theme is enlarged upon in the work of an American pastor, Eugene Peterson. His book *The Contemplative Pastor* is based on his work in a city parish in Maryland over twenty-nine years. In it he says that he wishes to redefine the meaning of the term 'pastor' by refusing the definitions of 'pastor' that the culture hands him. He claims that if he accepts the definitions which his culture offers him then he is rendered perfectly harmless, but he can rehabilitate his role by a redefinition of terms. One of the redefinitions he employs is the term 'busy'. He calls for 'unbusy' pastors, saying, 'How can I persuade a person to live by faith and not by works if I have to juggle my schedule constantly to make everything fit into place?'[4] His view is that many pastors are busy for two reasons, neither of them very good reasons. They are busy either because they are vain and cannot refuse any invitation by anybody to do anything, or because they are lazy and cannot order their diaries so that they have space for themselves or their families. He points out that the pastor who really inspires people is somebody who finds prayer and listening at the root of their being.

> The trick, of course, is to get to the calendar before anyone else does. I mark out the times for prayer, for reading, for leisure, for

the silence and solitude out of which creative work – prayer, preaching and listening – can issue. I find that when these central needs are met, there is plenty of time for everything else. ... If there is no time to nurture these essentials, I become a busy pastor, harassed and anxious, a whining, compulsive Martha instead of a contemplative Mary.[5]

His words are reminiscent of those of a neglected Anglican writer on preaching earlier this century, R. E. C. Browne. Browne was very concerned that the preacher of Christian doctrine should not attempt to expound a system of truth but hold doctrine 'by the whole movement of the mind in prayer', and, he concludes, 'All speech that moves men and women was minted when some man's mind was poised and still.'[6] For any of us in the Church, whether we are pastors or not, those moments when our minds are poised and still are usually very few, because all of us have accepted a culture which requires us to be continually active and doing. It is important to realize that what these writers say is important for the life of the professional pastor is equally so for anybody who has a public position and, indeed, any one of us in so far as our public persona is concerned. We need to be defined from within and from the mystical or contemplative spirit which carries us, rather than by the needs, perceptions and demands of the people whom we meet and maybe serve.

The second priority which we need to recover is the monastic spirit of place. The Rule of St Benedict and the vows which Benedictine monks and nuns take – and remember that a monk, especially in the early days, was not necessarily ordained – are different from the vows which are taken by a Franciscan or a Dominican. The Benedictine takes a vow of 'conversion of manners' and a vow of *stabilitas*. The vow of stability dedicates the Benedictine to be in that place with that community for the rest of their life. This vow and its vision of stable Christian community at a time of social disintegration laid the foundations for the beginning of the parochial system in Europe. I believe that Anglican parish life actually owes more to the Rule of St Benedict and its emphasis upon place than to the Franciscan way with its emphasis upon movement and availability. There has been a steady stream of reflection by both poets and theologians which speaks of this, beginning perhaps with Chaucer and his little portrait of a *Poure Persoun of a Toun* in *The*

Prologue to the Canterbury Tales. Chaucer's poor parson did not flee to a brotherhood in London or a chantry somewhere else where he might have some gracious, comfortable life doing what he thought was really spiritual, but actually lived with the people that he had.

> He sette not his benefice to hire
> And left his sheep encumbered in the mire
> And ran to London unto Sainte Paules
> To seeken him a chantery for soules,
> Or with a brotherhood to be withhold;
> But dwelt at home and kepte well his fold.[7]

This tradition continues through George Herbert in *The Country Parson* and Thomas Traherne, whose sense of place is graced with transcendental imagination. In the twentieth century it was well represented by W. H. Vanstone and the earlier poems of R. S. Thomas. Yet it is almost as if today there is a lack of confidence in this tradition, a lack of confidence in the simple act of being there and continuing to be there with the people, and the regular rhythm of prayer and pastoral care that being there requires. The parochial clergy, as well as almost every other type of profession, are increasingly subject to target-setting and achievable goals. Such mechanisms, important as they can be, must be set within the wider and less specific goal of simply being there, and, as Chaucer intimates, keeping well the fold.

The parish needs to be seen as the place where, above all else, the monastic rhythms are played out, and people and priest relate to each other and to God within these rhythms. Just as the monk or nun accepts the rule and the discipline, so the parish too is a school of the Lord's service. Parish priests and their people are witnesses, or should be, rather than missionaries. We are witnesses to what is present in our lives; we are not sent to discover something in another place which we think might be there or ought to be there. By maintaining a witness to the importance of place, we witness to something of the abiding love of God. We witness also to the abiding quality of that love for people who, in immediate terms, may not be those we find lovable or attractive. By means of a witness to the importance of stability and place, the church witnesses that God's abiding love is available. Such a witness is a warning against the view that the abiding love of God will more easily be found in places which are supposedly more spiritual. Anthony Russell writes of this spirit of place as far as the Anglican parochial ministry is concerned. He says:

> But the Church is not called to win the world for Christ; rather it is to help all to see that the world is already his and that the Kingdom is all about us. To do this in the same place for many years and to accept with equanimity the trials and limitations of such a community is a demanding role.[8]

A third item in this programme for the recovery of the mystical way in the Church is the recovery of wonder and delight as primary categories of living. Delight and wonder come first, and it is within that primary sense of wonder and delight that all Christian doctrine should be framed. Christian doctrines are not primarily intellectual ideas. To treat them as such eventually reduces them to the level of opinions. Christian doctrines derive from and set themselves within the wonder and delight which we have in God and he in us. The doctrine of the Trinity is a detailed expression of our wonder and delight at the nature and being of God. Without that, the doctrine of the Trinity becomes a sterile argument about the attempt to reconcile three and one. Without that deep sense of wonder the doctrine of the incarnation becomes nothing more than an argument about squaring human nature with Godhead. Within the context of wonder and delight which we have in Christ, that doctrine becomes a reality, a deeper and more profound reality. Without a sense of wonder and delight, faithfulness becomes a work, prayer becomes a duty, and we convey very little to those to whom we minister.

Moreover, we have spent far too much time in the Church up until now talking about commitment to God and the committed action which springs from that, rather than about the beauty and delight which we may have in God and he has in us. The consequences are physical, we tend to wear ourselves out in imitation of the constant activity of God, and philosophical, in that we come to believe that the will is the primary means by which human beings come to know or love God. We all become secret voluntarists. But God is better described as absolute beauty, and our primary means of knowing God is wonder or desire rather than willing or doing.

There are some indications that wonder and beauty are returning more to centre stage of the theological scene. The trail was blazed by the German theologian Hans Urs von Balthasar, but the torch has been taken up in this country by several others, including Patrick Sherry, Richard Harries the Bishop of Oxford, and now Michael Mayne. All of these thinkers are at the forefront of a recovery of theological categories of beauty as a means of understanding God, rather than 'commitment'. But it is hard work because we all believe we have to choose and do things rather than simply attend. Iris Murdoch led the way to the rediscovery of the place of attention and desire in our understanding of the human person when she wrote, 'We cure our faults by attention not by will', and it is interesting to realize that in actual fact most people spend more time in 'attention' than they do in following a commitment. Attention has a stronger priority than we realize. It is time we fashioned our theology around that instead of trying to persuade people to put their priorities somewhere else. Abraham Heschel, the Jewish mystic, spent a great deal of his life writing about the need for us to recover a deep sense of wonder, and made the point that this recovery is not something unnatural, as if we have to turn away from reason which is natural and strain after something else. Rather it is the other way round, and we have to allow a natural wonder to emerge from within us rather like the recovery of the writing on an old manuscript which has faded but which can be revealed by ultra violet light still to be there, only overwritten by some modern hand. He says:

> We do not have to discover the world of faith, we only have to recover it. It is not a terra incognita, an unknown land. It is a forgotten land and our relationship to God is like a palimpsest, a medieval manuscript which has faded and has been overwritten with the writing of modernity.[9]

Michael Mayne enlarges upon this theme in his book *This Sunrise of Wonder* where he suggests that there are a number of important 'triggers' to the recovery of a sense of wonder and delight.[10] He suggests that these 'triggers' include the experience of living in a new culture, the experience of finding ourselves in a situation where there is no guarantee that you have long to live, and the intensification of awareness that is provided by 'the framing of a moment in a painting or a poem'. All of these are, culturally speaking, moments which are often disregarded as of little importance, but they can open the doors of perception in us so that wonder becomes more important to us than success.

Further, I believe that we need to recover, as part of the programme for the recovery of the contemplative or mystical life, a 'negative capability'. This phrase comes from Keats. In one of his letters, Keats describes negative capability as occurring 'when man is capable of being in uncertainties, mysteries, doubts without any irritable reaching after fact and reason'.[11] He criticizes Coleridge for being unable to be content with imagery caught from 'the penetralium of mystery' because he was incapable of being content with half-knowledge. Our age and Coleridge are very similar – we are unable to be content with uncertainty, we do not have a large negative capability. Much contemporary theology lacks this capacity, but it is precisely because of such a lack that many honest men and women who are not in the Church but perhaps would like to be find themselves unable to be drawn further than the very edges of its life. They instinctively know something of the truth of Keats' insight but they see that in the Church we have abandoned that quest almost entirely.

Keats spoke of this 'negative capability' in a few fleeting phrases in his letters. The Anglican writer R. E. C. Browne gives it more substantial exposition in his advice to ministers of the word. He advises them to avoid what he calls 'schizophrenia':

> Schizophrenia is avoided by foreswearing all false simplifications so as to maintain the essential untidiness of mind consequent upon the acceptance of Christian doctrine. This essential untidiness is preserved by habitual refusal to come to definite conclusions where there can be none, without ever denying the value of either thought so limited or the forms of speech which embody such a doctrinal position. To have faith is not to possess or be possessed by an automatic activity; the life of faith is a way of accepting human limitations in the light of revelation which does not do away with them but makes them not only bearable but acceptable as the framework within which human maturity is achieved.[12]

A greater understanding of these words would not only enable the Church to represent the faith more truly to the outside world but also enable those outside the Church to respect the utterances of the Church and so release them to be drawn more closely into its contemplative embrace. Furthermore, a greater understanding of these words would be some indication of the desire of the Church to return to an earlier, more mystical style of expression of Christian truths rather than forcing all doctrine through the doors of a modernist understanding of reason, an understanding which many modernists, indeed many scientists, now feel compelled to abandon.

In addition to these four particular priorities there are two attitudes which today's pastor needs to recover if he or she is to bear the name of mystic. I speak of a different attitude to prayer and a different attitude to the study of scripture. It is I think clear that we need to recover a capacity to pray, but we need to learn to pray in a 'mystical' manner. Prayer is neither an asking nor is it a doing. To reduce it to such, as many contemporary manuals of prayer do, is to reduce it to the same status as anything else. It is to empty it of its 'doxological' quality. It then becomes simply another doing or asking, but with the simple distinction of being a 'spiritual' asking or doing. God is not so easily fooled. Prayer is not the same as everything else; it is a secret activity, something for which we must enter the innermost part of our being and then shut the door. For prayer is not our asking but rather our appropriation of the asking and receiving which goes on between the persons of the Trinity. It is our appropriation of the divine life. It is what Julian of Norwich called a 'beseeching', the nearest human parallel to which is the 'beseeching' which goes on between the different members of a family or the two partners in a long and happy marriage. Prayer is not something which we do but is rather something which is being done within us and within the whole creation by God, which we can either allow or turn away from. Prayer is a constant inner music which is playing within us and within the created order. We need to rediscover this music and allow it to be played within us. There is within each one of us a space where this music can be heard, a silence within which it is played.

Similarly with the reading of scripture. We need to recover an attitude to the reading of scripture where scripture is regarded as a text or the text of which we are a part. Rather than continuing to treat scripture as an objective reality or a record of objective history somewhere in the past, we must find once again something of the mystical and symbolic nature of scripture, and we must see ourselves as part of its ongoing narrative. Gerard Loughlin, in his book *Telling God's Story: Bible, Church and Narrative Theology*, says:

We must stress that baptism is entry into the story of Christ as the story of the Church. As the people who are learning to grow in the strength and shape of Christ, who are learning to live in the world as people who are not of the world, who are learning to speak a new language, the tongue of Pentecost.

He continues:

Salvation thus is no more and no less than entry into the narrative space of the Church. It is beginning to speak a new language in the company of those who are called to be friends by one who does not desert his friends even though they desert him.[13]

There are a number of things which need to be said about this programme for the recovery of contemplative priorities and attitudes in the Church's pastoral existence. First of all, this programme for the recovery of the 'mystical' person does away with the concept of the objective observer. Since the rise of the Enlightenment we have tended to believe that the essential human stance is that of the objective observer who can see what needs to be done and choose to do it. When this attitude is incorporated into religious faith it leads to the view that Christian truth, the scriptures, the life of the Church are all objective realities which can be observed and which the believer can then choose to believe or not believe. A more contemplative stance asks us to accept that we are not the objective observer but rather we are part of Christian truth, part of the ongoing life of the Church. To be restored to spiritual health we must let go of our ego-selves which say 'I can observe the scripture', 'I can tell you what Christian doctrine is', 'I can tell you what the Church is'. We must relinquish the objective observer if we are to live the mystical life.

Second, the spirituality which is tentatively described here is essentially a monastic spirituality. A monastic spirituality is one which values essences and seeks to preserve the essential place of praying, of loving and remembering within a community. Our identities are given us by prayer, by love and by remembering within the worshipping community and not by activity. Activity will certainly stem from prayer, from love and from remembering within community life, but identity will not be conferred upon us by activity. The monastic gift to the Church is the recognition of that truth. The monastic tradition should preserve something of the subversive characteristics of contemplative living within the Church. A further consequence should be that the parish is the monastery now. If you look for a place where the school of the Lord's service will be, it is within the parish where you are called to live with the brothers and sisters that God has given you. Every Anglican parish priest, if he or she wishes to remain true to what it is that is essential about being an Anglican parish priest, should read the Rule of St Benedict regularly as if in chapter with his or her monastic brothers and sisters. Then, lastly, I believe that the development of a monastic spirituality constitutes true evangelism. Such a development will draw the hesitant and the lost, those who recognize the virtue of spirituality but who have hitherto sought it in other religious traditions, despairing of the capacity of the Church to speak to them. By this contemplation, apparently so inert, apparently so inactive, apparently so unworldly, others will be slowly drawn to the *mysterium tremendum* at the heart of all things, the God of Isaac, of Jacob and of Jesus.

Most important, all of these items of a programme of recovery for a mystical Church will involve us in an exploration of the negative way. To maintain these priorities will challenge not simply the culture in which we are set, but some of the inherent attitudes which have coloured the mainstream exploration of the faith over the last hundred years or so. To uphold these priorities inevitably leads to a questioning of the modernism which has in many ways brought us to this point. It will bring us to a realization of the need to abandon what we have so far valued and so enter into a negativity of trust. To uphold these priorities will lead us through a *Via Negativa*, an *ascesis*, or a stripping, but eventually we will rediscover the beauty of ourselves as well as the beauty and loveliness of God. Sara Maitland entitles one of her books *A Big-Enough God?*[14] In it she asks Christians to set themselves free from the shackles which the older scientific view of the universe, what she and others call 'scientism', has placed around the doctrine of creation. She believes that acceptance of the apparent randomness of the created order is in fact an acceptance of the creativity of God, who is in the end far 'bigger' than our own conceptions of him. What she says about our attitudes to the creation can be applied to our attitudes to Christian doctrine and to the spiritual life in general. Her approach, she says, apparently gives us very little and takes away the old securities.

We have lost a knowable world. We have lost a servile science and an all-powerful deity. In exchange all I am offering you is a wild immeasurability, and a God who seems prepared to let the whole thing go on its own chaotic and random way. However I am certain that accepting all of this randomness and unknowability gives us more, if we dare receive it, than it takes away. I believe that what we have gained is complexity, freedom and loveliness.[15]

Adopting a set of mystical or contemplative priorities will involve us in the same sort of risk.

But in the end, what is at stake here is the whole question of how we act. The pastoral activity of the Church is in jeopardy because the sources of action are assumed to be within the life and work of the pastor rather than in God. The recovery of a contemplative pastoral practice within the Church depends upon a recovery of our capacity to live within the activity of God rather than assuming that action is ultimately ours. A number of postmodernist thinkers make the same point in different ways. For all of them the self is a form of fiction, a construct invented, ultimately, for hidden reasons of power and oppression. The deconstruction of the self by the postmodernist appears to result in a form of ethical nihilism, but for some this is no more than the revealing of the point of entry of the divine into the world. The absence of the self is the beginning of the presence of the transcendent. Mark McIntosh illustrates this from the work and writing of Edith Stein, the Jewish Carmelite nun who perished in Auschwitz in 1942. Edith Stein saw her vocation in political terms, but it was not a vocation to political action in the accepted sense. As McIntosh explains:

> Stein had a strong sense that 'the work of salvation takes place in obscurity and stillness. In the heart's quiet dialogue with God the living building blocks out of which the kingdom of God grows are prepared.' The self fulfils itself, achieves 'the highest elevation of the heart attainable by this co-suffering presence to others through surrender to God'; for in their hiddenness in God they are empowered to make their greatest act as persons, to 'radiate to other hearts the divine love that fills them and so participate in the perfection of all into unity in God'.[16]

McIntosh points out that Eckhart believed that the discovery of our true self is the discovery of our place in the trinitarian self-expression and self-giving.

A figure bearing many resemblances to Edith Stein is another Jew, Etty Hillesum, who also perished in Auschwitz, also because she

wished to give herself to God. Etty Hillesum's diary begins in self-
awareness and her preoccupation with herself as lover but
incomplete person. The diary ends with descriptions that are
almost impossible to read of those she served on the way to
Auschwitz and the profoundly moving prayers of one who had
abandoned herself to the loving of God at the root of the universe in
the face of the most terrible suffering. She talks about living as a
form of listening, an inward listening which then enables action, but
not before the self has been abandoned. She talks about making the
souls of those she is with as lodging places for God, but quite
unselfconsciously demonstrates that such a work is only possible
because it has first, or concurrently, been accomplished in her. Etty
describes her work as a sort of homecoming for God, a homecoming
in her and in those she works with. It is also a homecoming for
herself, one in which she is reconciled to herself and so is able to
'stay at home' as Chaucer's *Poore Persoun* was able to do.

To embark upon a contemplative pastoring, to call for a
contemplative Church, is identical to the call to live the trinitarian
existence, namely the self-abandonment which is necessary for the
life of God and the action of God to flow unnoticed into the world.
The postmodern deconstruction of the self is but the gateway to a
mystical participation in the divine activity. It reveals the working of
God.

7

Is Mysticism an Experience?

Within the search for the recovery of the Church from its colour blindness, there have been developments in our understanding of the mystical which mean that we are now faced with a unique opportunity, an unexpected but nonetheless welcome opportunity, whereby we can talk once again about the mystical aspects of Christianity without being regarded as eccentrics, or suspected of indulging in some private emotional experience to which no others can have access, or simply ignoring the constraints of the rational in religion. These are important developments allowing us to understand the mystical to be a normal, indeed a normative and central, component in the Christian life and allowing us to retrieve the colour of the mystical and spiritual life within the mainstream theological discourse of the Church. These developments have occurred within academic circles but can easily be related to the personal and pastoral.

Careful listening to those who speak or write about what are usually called 'mystical experiences' reveals that the question mark should not be placed over the word 'mystical', as if that were something which was, in itself, dubious and uncertain, but over the word 'experiences'. It is by no means certain that the mystical experiences of which people speak are really 'experiences' at all. That they are 'mystical', however, is not in doubt. Many pastors will be able to recall a conversation with a parishioner during which a mystical experience is described. While some of these descriptions employ religious imagery and phraseology, the most striking and authentic are those which describe a moment of what in conventional language would be described as 'heightened awareness', when the whole of the person's 'experience' comes alive in a new or more profound way. At these times there is no break with reality, indeed the reality is that which becomes increasingly present in some way. There is no account of angelic voices or visions, but the whole episode speaks in an unusual and profound way so that the individual concerned knows that they have been 'spoken to'. The research of the Alister Hardy Research Centre in the 1970s and 1980s revealed that a very large number of people can testify to episodes of this kind and that the people concerned are not necessarily regular churchgoers. Indeed the evidence shows that these mystical experiences are commonplace and we cannot expect that they will always be found within the regular life of the institutional churches.

What is also clear is that these so-called 'experiences' are closely related to what Baron von Hügel would have called 'inclusive' mysticism. For von Hugel, 'inclusive' mysticism was that sort of mysticism which described the whole world as being shot through with divine light, and where the person concerned knows that they are related to and united to that transfigured world. The clear implication of this is that all human experience has a potential for bearing God. In one sense mysticism could then be more properly described as an apprehension of existence at its greatest depth, or, perhaps, as it truly is rather than as it is perceived. Inclusive mysticism would also reject the view, or the implication, that there is a separate faculty or capacity in the human psyche by which God can be experienced. Not only is mysticism not an experience which separates the individual from reality (what von Hugel called 'exclusive' mysticism), but nor is it something which relies upon a special capacity for religious awareness which might be the particular property of some people. The spiritual, or 'awareness of the transcendent', is not separable from any part of existence but is contained within all that occurs and is communicated to human beings across the totality of their normal sensory experience. Rowan Williams, the Bishop of Monmouth, makes this clear:

> The Christian God is not an object in the universe and is not, therefore, a possible competitor for space in it. So it would not be true to say that we sometimes experience God 'neat' as it were, and sometimes at second-hand ... All our experience is experience of the world – of things, of persons. Experience of God is to learn to see these things and these persons in a certain context –

a context for which we can never find adequate description and which must never be reduced to being one item among others.[1]

Elsewhere Bishop Williams take issue with the idea that mysticism is a special sort of experience: 'Mysticism should not be taken to describe a cross-cultural, supra-credal specific experience, but a jumble of attempts to perceive how consciousness is drastically reconditioned by the living out in depth of a particular religious commitment.'[2]

Such a view can be substantiated from a careful study of the mystical texts themselves, but it is also inherent in the original use of the word mystical. One of the simple things that contemporary studies of the spiritual tradition has brought to light is the importance of using the word 'mystic' or 'mystical' in an older sense, a sense which we have largely lost but now need to recover. In the early days of the Christian faith the 'mysteries' of the faith were not some secret experiences which had been vouchsafed to the few, but were the liturgy and the regular reading of the scriptures which everybody attended. For originally the term 'mysticism' – which comes from the Greek *muo*, to hide – was nothing to do with special experiences of the divine which some people had and others did not, rather it was used to describe the sacred mysteries of the liturgy, those actions by which the *whole* people of God became aware of the divine reality. This use of the word is preserved in the term 'mystery plays' as in the York or Chester cycles of mystery plays, which, as anybody who has seen them will know, are anything but 'mysterious'!

This original meaning of the word has been lost. In our colour-blind Church the word 'mystical' is presumed to mean a special 'mystical experience'. By and large it has assumed that meaning since the work the work of William James and his 1902 Gifford Lectures *The Varieties of Religious Experience*. James' views are now seen to be deficient. Of late there has grown up an awareness that William James was himself a rationalist who sought to uphold the rationality of religion by describing it in terms of personal experience. Religious experience was, he believed, susceptible to scientific explanation and could be analysed and described as a phenomenon much like any other phenomenon in nature. For him this was the only way in which religion could receive any degree of acceptability in the modern world. Under this analysis, 'mysticism' was a particular type of religious experience whereby the soul was united with God, and James sought out quotations – often provided for him by others – from the mystical authors to support his case. Such a tactic delighted those who saw religion disappearing under the onslaught of purely rational or scientific categories, since it meant that religion could be rescued as acceptable and scientific. It even provided some degree of proof for the existence of God by means of what came to be called 'the proof of direct experience', even if this experience was limited to the very few who reached the heights of union with God. The rest of us could then at least linger on the foothills secure in the knowledge that all was well even if we could not see why it was well. In this way James played a role in rehabilitating the mysticism of the Christian tradition. It became that which proved the existence of the unseeable and rescued religious practice from the ever-intruding eyes of the rationalism of the present. Of course, the difficulty with this was that by so doing James reduced religion to inhabiting the realm of private experience. While intending this to be open to examination, he actually made it a matter of mere assertion, an area of life which was said to be there and so was said to prove a great deal. But in the end it was no more than a form of positivism of experience which, although intended to be subject to rationality, actually became publicly unexaminable. Ultimately it did no more than render religion safe because personal and private.

There are several fatal consequences to James' position. The first and most important is that the popular understanding of mysticism has been largely influenced by his views and when asked what is mysticism most people, intelligent Christians included, will say that it is a personal experience of union with the divine, or something very similar. Most people believe that mysticism is some sort of ineffable experience. The popular consequences of this were seen in the writings and activities of the 'beat generation' in the 1960s when people like Allen Ginsberg and Timothy Leary believed that because mysticism was essentially an experience then it could be attained just like any other experience, that is, by engaging in certain practices or techniques which, for example, might involve breathing or not breathing, diet, sex or the use of drugs. As soon as you placed the mystical in the category of experience then such a fall-out became inevitable.

A further, associated consequence is that all religions are then seen to have a mystical dimension which is basically the same, although their outward expressions might differ because of cultural and linguistic circumstances. This mystical residue came to be understood to be common to all religions and their ultimate safeguard. The practical consequences of this viewpoint have been considerable; it is a point of view which has lent philosophical support to the establishment of much inter-religious dialogue and the setting up of the World Parliament of Religions and a number of related bodies. This is not to say that dialogue is unnecessary or spurious, simply to say that much of it has been done on the basis that at rock bottom all religions are the same and that this is proved by the existence of mysticism in all of them. However, there has been a considerable scholarly reaction against such a view. We now take far more seriously than did William James the 'embodiment' of religious experiences, seeing the way they are expressed or 'embodied' in their social milieu as intrinsic to the experiences themselves. Social conditions or particular belief systems are not 'bolted on' to religious experiences as if they are essentially separable from them while the experiences remain essentially the same. Thus it can hardly be reckoned that the Buddhist under-standing of nirvana is the same as the Christian experience (if experience it is) of the negative way to God, since the understanding of 'God', and the social conditions which have given rise to those 'experiences', are, in each case, quite different. There is no 'common residue of experience' which is shared between the religions. There may be similarities but each religion possesses its own uniqueness. Increasingly dialogue is now being conducted on the basis of an affirmation of distinctiveness and the results are much more effective and long-lasting.

It is interesting and important to note in this regard that a similar shift has occurred within the confines of New Testament scholar-ship. Up to a decade or so ago it was generally reckoned that there were considerable links between the thinking of St Paul and the common religious inheritance of the Mediterranean world. This could be seen in Paul's use of vocabulary, if not concepts, borrowed, it was said, from the gnostic communities to be found in the great cities in which the gospel had to be understood. The usual examples given were those concerned with his description of the unity between the believer and Christ. The believer was *en Christo* and united to Christ in a way which would be readily understood by followers of Dionysius. This fuelled views of Paul as a 'secret' gnostic and reinforced a broad romantic view of the unity of all religions. Such a view was seen to be supported by a close examination of Pauline theology and so was understood to receive the imprimatur of the New Testament, when in fact it was no more than the product of the spirit of the age, an emergence of the *zeitgeist* within the hallowed portals of New Testament scholarship. It was a view which even allowed scholars of such standing as the German New Testament scholar Ernst Käsemann to believe that some of the impetus for the historical emphases of the Gospels was to correct the over-enthusiastic Pauline embrace of the common Mediterranean religious viewpoint. But once again the emphasis has shifted so that it is now clear that Paul's relationship was with Jewish rather than Mediterranean thinking and that his links with gnostic or proto-gnostic groups was very slight or non-existent. James Dunn, in his recent study, says:

> In the middle decades of the twentieth century a popular and much promoted view was that Paul derived the concept of the body of Christ from the gnostic primal man myth ... But the quest for a pre-Christian Gnostic primal man has now almost entirely been abandoned.[3]

Once again the demise of broadly liberal emphases, this time within the world of New Testament scholarship, allows the distinctiveness of the Christian allegiance within its Mediterranean setting to become more apparent.

A third consequence of the influence of the views of William James and his followers within the western Christian churches has been the explosion of the retreat movement and books and literature about 'spirituality'. Not all of this can, of course, be laid explicitly at the door of James himself, but once religion becomes defined as being essentially a matter of experience, or once the experiences of religion are regarded as those which provide its safeguard in a time of social change, then it becomes inevitable that the provision of devotional experiences through literature or special places will be at a premium. One of James' disciples was Evelyn Underhill, a founder member of and inspiration for the Anglican retreat movement, and the first Warden of one of the earliest Anglican retreat houses at Pleshey in Essex. Her books on mysticism and worship have influenced whole generations of clergy and lay people, but their expositions essentially rely upon the view that mysticism is an ineffable and unitive experience of the soul with the divine; and so the purpose of a religious retreat is to attempt to find or repeat such experiences. Grace Jantzen comments on this phenomenon by saying that 'with some notable exceptions books of popular spirituality treat prayer and spiritual exercises as strictly private, having to do with the relationship between the individual and the transcendent'.[4] She goes on to comment that these books have a common assumption in 'the privacy and subjectivity of religious experience, including mystical experience. By this privatisation of spirituality, the relation between it and social justice cannot be addressed.'[5] Thus William James has a great deal to answer for.

However, a sea change is occurring. It is now becoming clear, partly through a greater understanding of this essentially 'armchair' nature of William James' thinking, but also through a much more scholarly examination of the mystical texts themselves, that mysticism is not a minority religious phenomenon concerned with personal and private experiences of unity with the divine. The basic mystical texts of the Middle Ages simply do not support that view. Recent years have seen an explosion of scholarship on both sides of the Atlantic which enables us to come to such a conclusion and to know that this conclusion has increasing support from those in the academic world whose primary task it is to study the texts themselves. What has not happened is that this scholarly consensus has reached the everyday life of the churches. Pastors and teachers within the churches still largely hold to the Jamesian view that mysticism is a private matter. They thus reinforce the 'curious dichotomy' between theology and spirituality of which we have already spoken. Happily, however, things are beginning to change. The foremost British scholar engaged upon this work has been Professor Denys Turner. In a very important study entitled *The Darkness of God*, Turner spends a great deal of time analysing the purposes of medieval mystical texts themselves and their relationship to our understanding of religious experience. What are these texts for, and were they about experiences as we understand the word? He writes:

I wondered about this question because on the one hand there appeared to be a common, informal view around that the 'mystical' had something to do with the having of very

uncommon, privileged 'experiences'; and, on the other, because
when I read any of the Christian writers who were said to be
mystics I found that many of them – like Eckhart or the Author of
the Cloud of Unknowing – made no mention at all of any such
experiences and most of the rest who, like John of the Cross or
Teresa of Avila, did make mention of 'experiences' attached little
or no importance to them and certainly did not think the having of
them to be definitive of 'the mystical'.[6]

Turner comes to the conclusion that in fact the mystical writers were
talking about something very different from what we moderns mean
by 'mystical experiences' and, if anything, were sharply critical of
those who claimed to have them. Importantly, for our purposes,
Turner says,

> whereas our employment of the metaphors of 'inwardness' and
> 'ascent' appears to be tied in with the achievement and cultivation
> of a certain kind of experience – such as those recommended
> within the practice of what is called, nowadays, 'centring' or
> 'contemplative' prayer – the medieval employment of them was
> tied in with a critique of such religious experiences and practices.[7]

Such conclusions clearly have far-reaching implications for the
practice of Christianity in the modern world and we shall be
exploring some of those implications later in this book, but suffice it
to bear in mind at this point that Turner makes the important
assertion that much of what we moderns call mysticism is something
we have invented, and he wishes in his book to retrieve the medieval
tradition of apophatic or 'negative' mysticism. What he does not do
in his book is go on to say in any detail what this means for the life
of the Church as a whole and the place of mysticism in modern
ecclesial communities.

Turner's work is supplemented by that of Grace Jantzen. Whereas
Turner writes from the point of view of a philosopher simply
investigating the meaning of medieval philosophical texts, Jantzen
writes from a more distinctly feminist perspective. She comes to
essentially the same conclusion. 'It is relatively easy to show', she
writes, 'that the preoccupation of modern philosophers with the
alleged intense psychological states of consciousness is a serious
distortion of what the mystics themselves desired or held
important.'[8] Elsewhere she writes:

Contemporary philosophers are seduced by a particular picture of mysticism, inherited largely from William James ... what is hardly ever noticed is how little resemblance this bears to the things which preoccupied the medieval men and women whom they themselves would consider to be paradigm mystics.[9]

Professors Turner and Jantzen are, of course, not the only scholars who have found grounds, in their examination of what mysticism really meant in the Middle Ages, to reject the current popular consensus that it was something to do with ineffable experiences or heightened states of consciousness. Rowan Williams' study of Teresa of Avila is another example. Here Bishop Williams shows that whereas Teresa was entirely familiar with mystical experiences she never confuses them with the goal of the spiritual life. He writes:

> Teresa makes it very clear that the criteria of authenticity do not lie in the character of the experience itself but in how it is related to a pattern of concrete behaviour, the development of disposi-tions and decisions. There is no one kind of experience that declares itself at once to be an experience of God.[10]

The important thing to realize is that the reason why, as Bishop Williams puts it, 'there is no one kind of experience that declares itself at once to be an experience of God' is more to do with the nature of God than with the nature of experiences. God is essentially beyond experience. The starting-point for a real understanding of the nature of mysticism is not an analysis of the so-called experiences themselves, but a realization that God is not a separate reality, not even a 'spiritual' reality, if by those words we mean a spiritual reality which can be inspected by those endowed with 'spiritual experience' and so is susceptible to examination by the human consciousness. God is simply beyond human knowing. We have to accept that, however unpalatable it may appear at first sight. Once that is understood then mysticism actually becomes possible and indeed real for each one of us. If we continue to insist that mysticism is a kind of experience then it will either continually elude us or be regarded as the property of those who are spiritually equipped for such a thing. Either solution is dangerous: the one breeds atheism, the other breeds spiritual élitism. Once we understand that God is quite different, then, paradoxically, her difference becomes access-ible to all and so his reality becomes something which is either totally invisible or totally embedded in everything that is visible to us. This is the cornerstone upon which a modern understanding of mysticism becomes possible and which brings mysticism back within the reach of the people of God. William James' attempts to turn mysticism into an experience were, in the end, not only romantic and ill-founded, they were also élitist and had the opposite effect to what was intended.

Furthermore an understanding of God as essentially 'different' also enables us to understand the two strands of the mystical tradition as being far more closely related that we had realized. It is this enrichment of the Christian tradition which we so desperately need and which a richer understanding of the mystical tradition can bring. Broadly speaking the Christian mystical tradition has had two streams, the negative and the positive ways. The negative (or 'apophatic') way has stressed the total unknowability of God and the dark night of the senses as we approach his reality. Representatives of this tradition are Meister Eckhart and John of the Cross. The positive (or 'cataphatic') way stresses the impossible wonder of God and his transcendent beauty. This tradition is to be found represented in the works of Bernard of Clairvaux and Thomas Traherne among others. In the popular imagination the former, the negative, 'apophatic' way is regarded as normative. Mysticism is the negative way. But once we have discovered that God is not actually 'known' by either way, but both ways are forms of response to his actuality, then it becomes much more possible to see how both ways are linked and but the two sides of the same coin. The result is a return to a much deeper and wider understanding of the mystical nature of the Christian life. Instead of mysticism being seen to be no more than the negative way, and at that no more than an experiential negative way restricted to those who can achieve the heights of mystical achievement, the mystical life is understood as richer and deeper, comprising both negative and positive strands and based in a total re-enchantment of our selves, our speech and our action. In this way we shall also recover the psalmist's words, 'Darkness and light are both alike to thee. . .'.

Professor Turner reminds us how 'Thomas Aquinas made it very clear that in the end "we do not know what kind of being God is"'.[11] And because we do not know, because there is an un-knowability about God, human talk about God is inevitably indirect. When we attempt to speak of God one of two possibilities occurs.

Either our speech is blown apart by the immensity of God or we are struck dumb because we cannot speak of that which is God. Either we cannot stop speaking or we can say nothing at all. We either have to use every metaphor that is to hand or no metaphors at all. The only two possibilities for those who wish to speak about God are either too much speech or no speech at all. This is the source of all that the Church has called mysticism. But it is immediately plain that this is a very different thing from what most people call mysticism. For them, as we have already seen, mysticism is an exalted or ineffable state of consciousness, an experience of union with the divine, an assertion of a direct, rather than an indirect encounter, certainly an experience of some kind of union of the self with God. As Eckhart would say, this mistakes the way for the reality, for 'when you have found the way you have lost God'. It also places a barrier between ourselves and the mystical tradition and reduces almost to zero our chances of understanding what that tradition has been and consequently what that tradition has to become in our own age. If we wish to revive the possibilities of mysticism in our day then we have to allow ourselves either to be the carriers of so much speech that we cannot stop or the possibility that we cannot say anything at all.

Professor Turner would claim that this is what the tradition has said all along. He begins his study of the medieval mystics by defining the two terms 'apophatic' and 'cataphatic'. Apophatic theology, he says, is the sort of theology which is done against the background of human ignorance of the nature of God, not ignorance in the simple sense of 'not knowing anything about', as if mysticism were akin to not knowing anything, say, about the laws of physics or the way French verbs are conjugated, so much as ignorance in the sense of not being *able* to know anything about God, ignorance in the sense of moving into a totally different type of knowing, a knowing which is really a sort of 'unknowing' of who you and God are. 'It is', he says, 'the doing of theology in the light of the statement of Thomas Aquinas in the thirteenth century, that "we do not know what kind of being God is" '. Professor Turner then says:

> It follows from the *unknowability* of God that there is very little that can be *said* about God: or rather, since most theistic religions actually have a great number of things to say about God, what follows from the unknowability of God is that we can have very

little idea of what all these things said of God *mean*. And, strictly speaking, that is what 'apophaticism' asserts, as one can tell from its Greek etymology: *apophasis* is a Greek neologism for the breakdown of *speech*, which in face of the unknowability of God, falls infinitely short of the mark.

Professor Turner then goes on to speak of the positive or 'cataphatic' tradition of Christian mysticism:

> What then of the 'cataphatic'? The cataphatic is, we might say, the verbose element in theology, it is the Christian mind deploying all the resources of language in the effort to express something about God, and in that straining to speak, theology uses as many voices as it can. It is the cataphatic in theology which causes its metaphor-ridden character, causes it to borrow vocabularies by analogy from many another discourse, whether of science, literature, art, sex, politics, the law, the economy, family life, warfare, play, teaching, physiology, or whatever. It is its cataphatic tendencies which account for the sheer *heaviness* of theological language, its character of being linguistically *over-burdened*; it is the cataphatic which accounts for that fine *nimietas* of image which we may observe in the best theologies, for example in Julian of Norwich or Bernard of Clairvaux. For in its cataphatic mode, theology is, we might say, a kind of verbal riot, an anarchy of discourse in which anything goes.[12]

Professor Turner then speaks about the non-verbal vocabulary of theology, particularly in sacramental and liturgical action, music, architecture, dance, gesture and so on, thus demonstrating how all of 'theology' is a form of expressive discourse about God and is not, cannot be, confined to rational language. Indeed rational language is precisely not a form of theology because it implies that there is an object or an activity which can be seen and then rationally described. But as both scripture and Aquinas have told us, God cannot be seen. Thus all theology is best described as 'mystical' since it speaks, in different ways, of the hiddenness of God. It is only theology, whether apophatic or cataphatic (or to lengthen the list 'expressive'), if it presupposes the hiddenness of God. And it is for these very reasons that the original use of the word 'mystical' covered all of the activity of the Church, from the reading of scripture through the performance of the liturgy to the verbal expression of theology.

These were the sacred mysteries of the faith because it was by following all of them that the whole people of God became aware of the divine mystery of God's being.

These statements of Professor Turner are significant because they are the triggers for a number of important realizations. The first realization answers the question with which we began this chapter because it is the realization that mysticism is not an experience which can be 'described'. If God is essentially different then there can be no real describable experiences of him as if he were some sort of accessible reality which we could 'experience' in the same way that a theme park or a painting or a pop concert can be described to those people who were not fortunate enough to be there. If we listen carefully to those who speak or write about what are usually called 'mystical experiences' we will discover that the question mark should not be placed over the word 'mystical', as if that were something which was, in itself, dubious and uncertain, but over the word 'experiences'. It is by no means certain that the mystical experiences of which people speak are really 'experiences' at all. That they are 'mystical', however, is not in doubt.

The second realization is that all talk about God, whether it be apophatic or cataphatic, has to reckon with God's hiddenness if it is to be true to its own nature. We ought to have a problem in talking about God. This is not something which many of those involved in the public ministry of the Church today have readily understood. But thirdly, and more importantly, Professor Turner's statements enable us to realize that the positive and negative traditions of Christian mystical discourse are essentially related. They are both responses to the unknowability of God. The negative way does not represent the mystical way more thoroughly or more completely than the positive way. Neither way is more representative of mysticism than the other. There is no negative way which is somehow 'mystically superior' to the positive way. Both are the essential result of our incapacity to know what our language about God really means. This is a rebuke to those who have implied in their studies of mysticism that somehow the dark way is the more essential or even the more interesting. Indeed, a study of many of the Christian mystics will demonstrate that they are, in reality, protagonists of both ways. This was certainly true of Thomas Merton. He is both a cataphatic mystic in the sense that he has continually to write poetry and an apophatic mystic in the sense that at certain points he comes to an absolute stop and can say nothing. He writes a great deal, he goes on writing, he cannot stop writing, and one of the interesting things to biographers of Merton is the overwhelming evidence of the explosion in his life of metaphorical speech after a number of years in the monastery. He writes one diary then writes another one about the same thing, then writes another journal about that – he goes on and on, piling metaphor upon metaphor to talk about his experience of God. But then, at certain points, suddenly, he stops and says nothing. Before Mount Kanchenjunga he says nothing. Before the statues of the Buddha in Polonnaruwa he says nothing. And recent studies of Merton's unpublished writings demonstrate that there was an inner, dark way; a silent way behind all the verbal pyrotechnics of his published writings. Light dazzles just as much as darkness obscures. The two ways are not mutually exclusive and can and often do subsist within the same person.

One immediate and practical result of all this is that when we have to speak about God our sympathies must clearly be with the enthusiasts. In this case the enthusiasts are those who find that they have to use metaphor upon metaphor upon metaphor upon metaphor, like Bernard of Clairvaux or Thomas Traherne from the twelfth and seventeenth centuries, or like Annie Dillard, one of the present-day inheritors of the cataphatic mystical tradition. Or they are the enthusiasts who find they cannot use any language at all because they have been overwhelmed by the reality of which they try to speak and so find that all language is totally inadequate. Examples of these are Eckhart and the Author of *The Cloud of Unknowing*, or Paul Celan and R. S. Thomas in our own day. All of them are right. Both types of enthusiasts are overwhelmed, one by the need to speak in a constant stream of metaphor, the other by the need to be silent. These two enthusiasts are twin sisters. The health of the Church requires that these twin sisters should be rehabilitated and once again allowed to walk together. There is a deep correspondence between those who cannot stop talking about God and those who are forced to stop talking about God because they cannot find any language which is adequate. So in that sense 'the darkness and the light are both alike to thee'.[13]

8
Mysticism and the Postmodern

One of the consequences of studying the medieval mystics is the realization that they are not very 'modern'. They are not like us. Modern people are preoccupied with experience and place a very high value on the savouring, almost the collecting, of experiences in very many walks of life. Religion is part of this. 'Being religious' is, for modern people, a way of life in which religious experience is defining. The religious way of life consists of living in such a way that experience in worship is central and much of the late twentieth-century's capacity to accept religion – as over against the rejection of religion which characterized the earlier part of the century – was due to the claim that religion is such an experience. So religion 'fits in' with the twentieth-century's capacity to accept anything as valid provided that those who experience it find it acceptable or useful or helpful in their daily life. As we pointed out in an earlier chapter, religion becomes problematic for modern men and women at exactly that point when, for various reasons, their experience of it becomes problematic. When it becomes less than the experience they wanted, or when it ceases to be an experience as they define it, it is questioned. It is then only a matter of time before such a disappointing form of religion is abandoned. Indeed such is the power of religious experience over the minds of many in the Church, even those who are in responsible positions, that almost any form of experimentation is allowed and even encouraged provided that it gives the participants what is generally understood to be an experience of God. This is so even when such experimentation breaks with very long-standing liturgical traditions. In this way experience defines worship rather than vice versa.

In this sense medieval mysticism is not modern because it developed and held its place in the life of the Church precisely because it was not such an experience. Indeed it was clearly understood to provide a critique of these experiences. This means that reading the mystics is quite difficult for modern Christians. They attempt to assimilate them into their own experientialist patterns and impute to the mystics an experience of God which the mystics themselves believed was an obstacle to understanding God. If they cannot assimilate them into their own experientialist patterns they reject them as being élitist. Consequently the gap between modern men and women and the mystical tradition is very wide and has been widened by such readings of mysticism as those provided by Professor Turner. If the mystics were not experientialists as we had supposed, then does not that simply widen the gap between us and them? Professor Turner himself admits his interpretation makes the mystics seem less attractive to us. He says:

> The mystics I discuss may seem to acquire, as a result, a rather more austere, spare, 'reduced' physiognomy than they appeared formerly to possess. But I am afraid I think it more important to dislike these authors, if we must, for what they are than to like them for what they are not.[1]

This realization might, in fact, remove the mystical tradition from our grasp were it not for the arrival of the postmodern. For the modern, with its accent on the individual self and on the experiences of the individual self, cannot retrieve the genuine mystical tradition in its own terms. It can only retrieve what the modern mind believes was the mysical tradition. Our modern presuppositions are so engaged with the self and its possessions that we cannot engage with a tradition in which there is no real sense of self as we have developed it. In the course of his study of the medieval mystics Professor Turner says that he came to realize that they were working not just with an apophatic theology but also with an apophatic anthropology, that their sense of 'self' was, at least from the modern perspective, very underdeveloped.

> With Eckhart, the *Cloud* author and with John of the Cross, the problem became inescapable of what significance their practical strictures of a 'self-denial' and a detachment had for what we think of, if there is any one thing that we think of, as being 'the

self'. . . . All three in *some* sense deny that I am 'a self' . . . Nor are they alone in this, Julian of Norwich, Catherine of Genoa and Teresa of Avila being three others who say the same.[2]

This might appear to be disastrous. Certainly from the point of view of a 'modern' Church, wedded to a substantial view of the self and the importance of self-fulfilment and the place of the experiences of the self in the economy of things, it is a disaster. It simply places the mystical tradition even further out of reach and increases the distance that modern Christians have to travel before they can even begin to understand what such people are saying. It also has the reverse effect of convincing modern Christians that they are in fact even more right than they thought they were, that they are the representatives of progress and development, while the mystics were, of course, underdeveloped or unaware of the possibilities contained in human nature. They can, therefore, be of no earthly use in the task of the Church today.

But what if the modern perspective is, even in the slightest degree, wrong? What if, even in the smallest way, the modern perspective does not contain all that needs to be said? What if the modern way of looking at things is not the truth we have waited for so long but is simply a metaphor for our self-understanding that in the end does not and cannot bear long-term scrutiny? What happens when the modern begins to dissolve into the postmodern? It would, of course, depend on what the postmodern tendency is, but it should be reasonably clear by now that postmodernism involves a 'decentring' of the self, an awareness that the self is not a distinguishable reality which interprets and validates all other realities. Indeed the post-modern perspective on things is a way of bringing the over-inflated view of the self into the light of reality; a way of deconstruction so that a proper humility about the place of the self is restored. In that sense the acceptance of postmodernism might well be able to set us free to see more clearly the true nature of the mysticism of the past. If that mysticism itself relied upon a decentring of the self in order for God to be available to faith, then a contemporary philosophical understanding which relies upon a similar decentring should provide the opportunity for that earlier mysticism to take on its true colours and become available to contemporary men and women in a way which it has not before. Indeed, if one of the functions of mysticism in medieval society was precisely to free believers from the seduction of the self, then postmodernism should perform the same function in contemporary western civilization. Denys Turner hints at such in his study: '[These] remarks hint at the possibility that certain quite contemporary developments in Western thought, associated with "post-modernism", contain a revival of that awareness of the "deconstructive" potential of human thought and language which so characterised classical medieval apophaticism.'[3]

Turner's thesis is that the popular understanding of mysticism as being a form of personal, unitive experience of God is a modern invention. We have poured into the classical understanding of mysticism a modern view of religion as a form of experience. But what the classical authors were doing was using the language of negativity to bring those who used it to an awareness of the impossibility of talking about God in the same way that you can talk about anything else. The traditional language of mysticism was therefore a form of deconstruction of religion, a constant practice of distance or detachment from the reality of God by which the proper reality of God was revealed. The mystics were aware, as almost nobody else, that using language about God in such a way as to suggest that God can be described in the way that anything else can be described actually diminishes God. Such a use of language might appear to make God too available, it might persuade its users that they were using language in such a way that the reality of God was more accessible than was really the case. It is a particular temptation in times when faith is apparently in crisis to use language in this way. If belief in God is in difficulty then talking about God as if he were a present reality becomes more commonplace. The mystics insisted, however, that the language we use has to be such as to preserve God's difference, her distinctiveness. God is not a commonplace. And it is precisely this that the postmodern theologian wants to do. Such a theologian wishes to undermine the capacity of theological language to rest in fundamentals of any kind in order that we should rest more securely in God alone. For such a theologian all proper theology is necessarily imperfect. It is always at one remove from its object and so its object is not an object at all. It is only by constant recognition of this that the very reality of God can be preserved as such. If God is to be God then all talk about her is inadequate. What Turner calls the dialectics of the negative tradition preserves the very 'Godness' of God. What the postmodern theologian is doing in his or her desire to decentre or destabilize the self, or to undermine the grand narratives of the past, is precisely the same. He or she is, if he or she is a believer, attempting to rescue the Godness of God from the systematic and commonplace patterns of expression which hide her. As Turner says:

> It is within the dialectics of negativity and in the metaphors of those dialectics that the common ground between mediaeval apophatic theology and contemporary intellectual concerns is more likely to be found. ... in the mediaeval apophaticist's obedience to the conditions under which language as such breaks down into disorder, in his subtle sense of the power of that which is inaccessible to language to determine what language expresses, *therefore in the character of discourse as deconstruction* there is much to arouse the contemporary mind.[4] (my italics)

In short, then, we can see in the arrival of postmodernism an opportunity for the Church rather than a crisis. The arrival of postmodernism, while at first sight appearing to undermine the certainties upon which the exposition of the faith relies, certainties such as a sense of self-identity, a personal grasp of the tenets of belief by the individual soul and a pattern of understanding of God's dealings with humanity in which the individual can feel secure, presents the Christian community with the opportunity to restate its faith with an integrity it has not been able to possess for several hundred years. No longer should it feel the need to state the faith in such a way as only rational people can understand; no longer does human reason have to be the sole guardian of a reasonable faith; no longer are pre-modern realities automatically assumed to be superstitious realities. The modern, with its use of reason, can take its place as one of the tools by which faith is interpreted and expressed, one of the metaphors which are available for the exposition of the faith, one of the ways in which we come to understanding, but not, any longer, the sole way. Once more the metaphoric, the allusive, what Emily Dickinson calls 'the slant', can come into play as they did in the earlier periods of the faith.

It is very difficult for theologians to take this much more fluid postmodern situation on board, but it does, when accepted, bring a number of advantages. In speaking of the loss of the old sense of self which the Enlightenment gave us, Sara Maitland reminds us that we should not mourn its loss too much, for a different view of person-hood, one which she calls a 'co-creative, deeply social, integrative view', should enable us to make better sense of the Christian doctrines such as the incarnation and the resurrection, and help us to understand what is really meant by what Paul calls 'incorporation into Christ'. There are, of course, losses when the old essentialist view of the self is abandoned, but they are hardly to be mourned.

> We have lost an infantile sense of passivity; we have lost the splendid conviction that the whole universe is a cot in which we are tucked safely and rocked tenderly ... We have lost both Platonic and Cartesian dualisms – which have allowed us, directly and indirectly, to mess up the planet. ... We have lost the romantic and arrogant notion of ourselves as solitary travellers in an alien land, the Great White Hunter, the Nimrod of the cosmos, who eventually, hung with trophies, will go *home* to heaven and patronize the angels. ... We have lost a mechanical saviour doll...[5]

What we should also lose is an infantilized view of mysticism as providing us with some form of self-improvement or proximity to God and release us into a true mysticism in which a proper relationship between the transcendent creator and the creature is preserved. But this might prove more difficult than we thought.

Professor Turner is right then to suggest that in the study of medieval apophaticism 'there is much to arouse the contemporary mind', for a large number of contemporary postmodern writers have been fascinated by the negative way. But what Turner hints at as a possibility with proper academic caution, others have rushed to prove as a certainty and in the rush have forgotten a number of central things. Whereas it is true that the contemporary breakdown of the modernist viewpoint should enable the Church to reach back into the past and retrieve a number of ways of understanding God which have been covered over by the rationalism of the past two hundred years or so, and we have already seen how postmodernism can assist the Church in its exposition of the nature of the self and the doctrine of the Trinity, the real question is whether the postmodern theologian can also avoid the scylla of nihilism while still seriously escaping from the charybdis of the clutches of his or her modernist past. Can postmodern theologians, having understood the necessity to deconstruct the self or the selfishness of experience as being simply one more form of imperialism, still talk about God with any conviction? Are they ready to affirm that there is a reality to the notion of God once all talk about her has been properly deconstructed? Is there anything behind the negative way they so ardently espouse, or is their deconstruction no more than a novel means of baptizing the nihilism of the modern world? The emphasis on the negative way in medieval times was to preserve God as God, to prevent him being reduced to that which was less than God. It could be argued that the purpose of the deconstructionist in contemporary thinking is somewhat different; it is to disallow dominance, the dominance of a so-called invincible reason, or whatever other imperialism we are said to suffer from. Are these two things the same? Can deconstructionist thinking be accorded the same degree of honour in the Christian tradition as the thinking of those in the mainstream of classical mysticism? The question is whether contemporary deconstructionism and the mystical way as properly understood, are, or are not, the same. Are the parallels between what, say, Meister Eckhart was doing in the thirteenth century and what the postmodernist thinker in the late twentieth century was attempting to do as he or she talked of 'decentring' the 'grand narratives' of the Church, sufficient to say that what happened then is now happening all over again?

Such a question might at first sound like no more than a cleverness, an academic exercise which will do no more than weary the brain; but there is a great deal more than mere thinking at stake. The point is that a number of contemporary religious thinkers have become convinced that the traditional orthodoxies of the Church have lost their credibility. What they see themselves doing is restoring the credibility of religion because orthodox religious faith has, it is said, been used in the past to justify oppression and stifle religious freedom. It is claimed that orthodoxy of belief and practice are inevitably male inventions. They perpetuate patterns and systems of belief used by the male establishments of the past to divide, to rule and to control. By these lights postmodernism is an attempt to wrest theology from the control of the hierarchical Church and give it back to the people, especially women, from whom it has been stolen. Meanwhile mysticisms, it is said, were those movements which protested against such controls. Mystics were from the female side of the Church as well as from the poorer classes, and it is they who were persecuted by the authorities not just for attempting to restate the nature of the faith but also for challenging authority. The fact that in the late twentieth century mysticism and postmodernism were once more united in a battle against the hierarchical nature of

Christian orthodoxy is seen as no more than a continuation of an ancient battle. Nor is this thought to be a meaningless academic battle. It is seen to be a battle for a Christian freedom, an assertion of a form of evangelical faith which will allow people to reaffirm a faith in God which is primarily theirs, which has not been given to them by the grand narratives of the past.

The outstanding proponent of this point of view is the writer and theologian Don Cupitt. In his book *Mysticism after Modernity*, Cupitt's basic premiss is that we should not lament the demise, during the latter half of the twentieth century, of the grand narratives of light and truth which have served us so far. They are, he claims, but a modern invention. We should not be afraid, but rather rejoice for these latter days are but the birth pangs of the new age, and we should leap with joy from the foundering ship of faith into the sea of relativism by which we are surrounded. When we do so we shall discover that the apparent darkness of modern world is the same darkness as was described by the classical mystics of the Christian tradition. The emptiness of the postmodern condition is nothing but the dark night of the soul returned to us in a new form. Cupitt is well aware that classical mysticism cannot be classified as an 'experience' in the modern sense of the term. Like Professor Turner and a number of others he is deeply critical of early twentieth-century attempts to rehabilitate mysticism as a form of experience. This he says obscures the deliberately subversive agenda of the classical 'mystic' by wrapping him or her in some form of 'psychic' package:

> All this was obscured in the period 1790–1970, when our Modern conception of mysticism was developed. The mystics were then repackaged as psychic sensitives who had wonderful, wonderful experiences that confirmed the truth of orthodoxy! ... They were being canonised in retrospect by the same System which had persecuted them. Their posthumous rehabilitation did the mystics no good at all, and greatly cnfused the definition of mysticism.[6]

It is certainly an overstatement to say that the modern rehabilitation of the mystical life by William James and Evelyn Underhill was a 'canonization' of the medieval mystics by 'the System which had persecuted them', especially as much of the Church of their day remained either ignorant or sceptical of their writings; but Cupitt's thesis that classical mysticism was something generated from below in the life of the Church and in the face of the hierarchy would receive some endorsement from a number of well-regarded scholars. What is more problematic is whether, notwithstanding Cupitt's awareness that classical mysticism cannot be equated with the contemporary quest for religious experience, he understands just how radical the medieval mystical way was. Does he understand that or is his exposition of mysticism no more than an assimilation of what was happening into his own modernist preconceptions? Does even he, who readily relates the mysticism of Meister Eckhart to the postmodern phenomenon, really grasp the difference that there is between Eckhart and our own ways of thinking?

There are certainly some singular features in his account of the relationship between medieval mysticism and postmodernity, many of them sudden and striking insights, but whether his overall picture is radical and postmodern enough is very unclear. Cupitt asks us to welcome the breakdown of the modern way of understanding with joyful acceptance. To do this is to enter into what he calls the 'mysticism of secondariness'. 'Secondariness' is a good thing because it is all we have left to us now. There are no primary things any more. There is no author for a text because a text, such as a novel or a poem, is the product of a set of circumstances; there is no God because the God we have believed in is the product of the institution, and so on. There are no 'primary' things, no real things, only impressions, phenomena, what he calls 'secondariness'.

> This mysticism of secondariness is a form of religious consciousness that actively rejoices in and affirms all the features of the postmodern condition. ... [It] is a thoroughgoing and free-floating relativism embraced with rapturous joy. The older 'platonic' kind of mysticism was usually claimed to be *noetic* – by which I mean that people saw religious experience as a special supernatural way of knowing something Higher that was itself correspondingly super-natural. ... But now, with the end of metaphysics and two-worlds dualism, we should give up the idea that mystical consciousness is noetic. That is we give up the idea that mysticism is a special wordless way of intuitively knowing the things of another and higher world. We may discover that we simply do not wish to go *beyond*.[7]

Cupitt goes on to claim that this 'thoroughgoing and free-floating relativism' is precisely what energized the original mystical tradition especially as represented by Meister Eckhart. Eckhart, declares

Cupitt, 'skips all the way from Thomas Aquinas to the mysticism of secondariness' and arrives there 'when his quest for perfect purity of heart leads him to a disinterested and joyful affirmation of the gratuitous outpouring of life in the present moment'.[8]

Cupitt expands this by saying that Eckhart took the old concept of eternity, the old metaphysical belief in the world above, and concertinaed this belief into the 'now moment' of human experience. This programme is very much the same as that of the radical theologian. Just as Eckhart did then, so now in our day the radical theologian attempts to ' ''de-objectivise'' or ''demythologise'' the spread-out religious System, telescoping it all back down into the felt relation to the forthcoming of life in the Now'.[9] Cupitt concludes by claiming that to accept this view of mysticism is to release oneself into religious happiness and into the 'eternity' of the non-realism of God.

Cupitt's programme has superficial attractions. Above all it relates the religious tradition to contemporary experience and vocabulary. His talk about 'surfing' reality as being exactly what Eckhart intended is a way of relating the mystical to the contemporary scene and the way people now feel about things. It is, in effect, a form of contemporary evangelism. Effectively he says that the modern experience of emptiness and directionlessness is exactly what we are supposed to experience when the mystics talk to us about the negative way to God. It is a form of baptism of the modern, or at least a religious interpretation of the modern, which many find appealing. In particular his criticism of the systematic doctrinal hold that the Church appears to have held over people's lives does ring a number of bells with the current generation. Many welcome his radical affirmation of the religious value of emptiness of today. On the way, however, he takes a number of great and dazzling religious strides. He rejects not just the realism of God but also the conclusions of so many thinkers who have laboured in the same vineyard that one begins to wonder when his radical rejection of them – even of those who were once regarded by him as the means towards a deeper and more radical theology – will come to an end. Kierkegaard, the Danish theologian, is well known for his espousal of the otherness of God, but, significantly, Cupitt turns aside from his thinking.

> It is objected at this point that ... I should rather be guided by Kierkegaard's phrase 'the infinite qualitative difference,' and

should see the Infinite as a qualitatively different order, or mode, of being ... Very well: but a move of this type, by making God the wholly Other, only makes matters worse. God becomes absolutely or metaphysically unknowable and hidden from us, an idea that cannot even be stated without intolerable paradox, and that creates an effect of truly dreadful religious despair and frustration.[10]

But it is precisely this hiddenness and the intolerable paradox of talking about it that Eckhart, and those who, like him, draw their inspiration from Pseudo-Dionysius, embraces. It is precisely this depth of paradox and radical otherness that Aquinas talks about when he says that 'We do not know what kind of being God is'. Is the Eckhart that Cupitt so readily endorses the real Eckhart or a projection into his texts of Cupitt's rather timid preconceptions?

It is not just Kierkegaard that Cupitt turns away from. He also turns away from the nuanced discussions of Michel de Certeau, the French scholar of late medieval mysticism, in favour of what appears to be a simplistic view of the development of Christianity divided between the two conflicting strands 'priestly and institutional'.[11] And then, almost as it were without blinking, he also turns away from Jacques Derrida's view of Eckhart. Although Derrida, one of the leading French postmodernists, is at first tempted by the parallels between his own nihilistic thinking and that of Eckhart, he finally rejects him, since, he says, Eckhart's way eventually leads us back to a belief in God as somehow 'existing'. Eckhart is not radical enough because, in the end, however impossible he found it to talk about God, he is still an orthodox believer. Derrida, of course, at this point accurately reflects the consensus view of Eckhart scholarship, but Cupitt is more reckless. He says, 'To return Eckhart to orthodoxy is surely to misunderstand him. Orthodoxy is a legal construction. It presents a vocabulary and a complex system of rules, written and unwritten, governing what and may not be said in it.'[12] We are off once again into a set of preconceptions which are far more the product of Cupitt's own concerns about the legal nature of orthodoxy than the result of careful study of what it was that Eckhart actually said and believed. To claim that orthodoxy for Eckhart was a 'legal construction' is hardly scholarly, let alone true. At this point Derrida has the sharper insights and was right to turn away from parallels between his own thinking and that of Eckhart because he recognized that Eckhart was not a twentieth-century nihilist like himself but was a believer.

What seems to be happening here is that Cupitt is confusing two things. He is confusing his opposition to what he calls 'objectivist' theology with the negative way of classical mysticism. In an important article on Cupitt's understanding of mysticism, Denys Turner points out that Cupitt totally underestimates the radical nature of classical mysticism. 'I do not think', he says, 'that Cupitt's polemic against theological "objectivism" even begins to get to grips with the resolute apophaticisms of the medieval theological, mystical and spiritual traditions.'[13] Turner points out that within this medieval tradition God is not any kind of thing because he is the very cause of all that exists including ourselves. And if God cannot be defined objectively, nor can he be defined subjectively. He simply eludes all our categories, subjective as well as objective, by the very fact that he is God. In other words the medieval mystics never thought that God was some sort of objective reality in the first place. Their negative mysticism was not a protest against the same objectivism that Cupitt is railing against – that is a product of his own consciousness. So Cupitt is using negative theology to support his own late twentieth-century campaign against the objective reality of God in a way which the medievals would not have understood or would have found impossible to accept if they had. As Turner says:

> The common thread which may be identified as running between the speculative mysticisms of the Pseudo-Dionysius, Thomas Aquinas, Bonaventure and Eckhart – in spite of their many and very great differences from one another – is to be found not, it must be said, in their critique simply of 'theological objectivism'.[14]

What they are truly critical of, Turner suggests, is some sort of view whereby God and the human, or God and the self, are in competition with one another, and it is in this insight that they are close to the postmodern thinker who similarly wishes to remove competition between God and the self in a truly 'decentred' universe. The very fact that Cupitt's thinking is dominated by the sense of competition which the medievals and the truly postmoderns wish to undermine, a sense of competition in which he constantly has to dethrone God or orthodoxy or whatever other tyranny he can fix upon, shows that he is not really postmodern at all, but is still caught in the modernist mind set. Turner even hints that the real aim of the medieval mystic was to take people out of a mind set which rests either in a naive non-realism or in a naive realism about God, in other words just the position which Cupitt himself adopts! For the battle in Cupitt's mind between objectivism and non-realism about God is really no more than the modernist battle writ large. It is, broadly speaking, the struggle of the twentieth century between 'I' and God, from which both the medieval mystic and the postmodern theologian are attempting to free us. As Turner says:

> For if the medieval mystic and the contemporary critic of modernity share anything in common, it is in the shared rejection of the 'modernist's' assumption of a 'centred' universe, in which God and the human have to compete for the autonomy spot.[15]

Cupitt's attempt, therefore, to enlist the medieval mystics in his support fails because the mystics are themselves more radically postmodern than Cupitt himself. His concern is with the conflict between the objective reality of God and the capacity of human beings to be human. He wishes to dethrone what he calls the theological objectivism of God and allows human self-consciousness to expand and to take up the space that he believed God once occupied. That becomes clear in the last sections of *Mysticism after Modernity* where he talks about the need for humans who are free, with the apparent aid of Eckhartian thinking, of the objective reality of God, to rediscover the 'happiness' and 'eternity' that is their birthright. In this way he remains cast in the modernist viewpoint from which he claims to escape. He constantly speaks of the capacity of the human person to experience the 'happiness' and 'eternity' which he claims are the true legacy of the mystical way. This means that still, for Cupitt, mysticism is a form of experience. His descriptions of mystical happiness are really no more than the old Jamesian categories of mystical experience rephrased in the language of the late twentieth century. He cannot accept the radical decentring of the human person which the apophatic tradition demands. When he says, 'I am grateful for the sheer gratuitousness of everything. I feel spiritually liberated, cleansed, unaccountable, carefree, floating. That existence is purposeless is to me religiously wonderful...',[16] we know that what Cupitt cannot seem to free himself from is the 'I' of his experience, and it is at this point that he is vulnerable. Professor Turner points out that in Eckhart *all* of our

desires are affected by his decentring of the self, even love.
Detachment is a more important virtue than love, for without
detachment love does not function properly. Without such a
detachment we are not loving the true God but a god of our own
invention, one we have placed in existence to have mastery over us.
There is, unfortunately, little in Cupitt's account about detachment
and a very great deal about what the results of his mystical way
might be for 'me'. As Turner reminds us, Eckhart stands in strong
contrast to all of this:

> Then how should I love God? You should love God unspiritually,
> that is, your soul should be unspiritual and stripped of all
> spirituality, for so long as your soul has a spirit's form, it has
> images, and so long as it has images, it has a medium, and so long
> as it has a medium it is not unity or simplicity.[17]

Or, as he says elsewhere, 'Whoever is seeking God by ways is
finding ways and losing God, who in ways is hidden.'[18]

It is worth at this point quoting the whole of Professor Turner's
conclusions about Cupitt's attempt to enlist the medieval mystical
tradition in the search for a contemporary religious awareness. This
is a laudable aim, certainly, but it fails because Cupitt himself is
insufficiently 'postmodern'. Turner writes:

> My argument, therefore, is that a theological discourse which
> embodies the insights of the medieval 'mystic' knows itself to be
> the decentred language of a decentred world, a discourse which is
> above all a moment of 'unknowing' and mystery in a contingent
> and semantically unstable world. As such, theological language
> will be seen primarily as a language of criticism. For in that world
> humans exhibit the opposed, ideological instinct to stabilize their
> universe upon absolute sources and referents of meaning, upon
> idolatrous myths, whether of God or of the human. It is a false
> theological instinct which provokes a theologian to displace a
> God at the centre on the assumption that what is opened up
> thereby is a gap which the human has to fill. This is a false
> theological instinct not because, after all, it is God who belongs at
> the centre, but because, although there is a God on whom all
> depends, there cannot possibly be any language in which to
> embody the meaning and significance of that centrality of God.
> Theological language therefore knows itself to consist in failure,

for it knows itself in its ultimate 'unknowing'; and in knowing that, it knows all language ultimately to fail, for theological language is but the ultimacy of all language. Hence also, it knows the name of all discourses, whether of politics, science, theology or spirituality premissed upon a pretentious claim to know, premissed upon *any* privileged 'centredness': it is the name of 'idolatry'. And so the very best reason why the God Cupitt takes leave of does not exist is that his 'autonomous consciousness' does not exist either. Both are idolatrous illusions, for we do not live in the sort of universe in which either can exist.[19]

One of the purposes of this chapter has been to demonstrate that if we are to take the opportunity afforded by the break up of the modernist viewpoint to retrieve something of the importance and centrality of the mystical life for the Church to day, a task which is essential if we are truly to engage with the contemporary world and speak the truth of the gospel to it, then we have to recognize that there are a number of pitfalls on the way. Cupitt's attempt is correct but his conclusions are inadequate simply because he does not see what Turner calls the 'contingent and semantically unstable world' in which we live as being exactly that. He has not come to an interior realization of the impermanence of modernity and of its innate capacity to fragment into unreality at the critical point. This has the consequence that his understanding of the language we must use when talking about God is similarly skewed. All of his attempts to talk about the final condition in which he is left are strangely self-indulgent. They contrast vividly with the two traditions of the mystical way, the cataphatic and the apophatic, in which either too much is said or very little is said at all. Cupitt has not taken the *unreality* of God seriously enough. He has not taken the unreality of God seriously enough to force him into mystical language, certainly into the rigorous mystical language of negativity which is shown in Eckhart and those who follow him or into the stream of language such as is used by Bernard or Thomas Traherne where metaphor after metaphor cannot diminish the distance or encompass the infinite closeness which there is between God and the soul.

There is one last point to make. What has become clear from this discussion of Don Cupitt and his critics is this, that there is now a condition of the human psyche in the western Christian tradition which does allow some parallels to exist and some links to be made between ourselves and the medieval mystical tradition. The way is clear now. That tradition is not entirely lost, rather it has been obscured for the last two or three hundred years. It went underground and was lived, perhaps on the fringes of the institutional Church, kept alive by the ordinary person in the pew; kept alive, perhaps most of all and most quietly, within the much despised, apparently 'withdrawn' monastic tradition; kept alive, perhaps, within the poetic and literary traditions of the West by the apparently disenchanted poets of the nineteenth and twentieth centuries. But now there is a real opportunity to banish the idolatries of those years, idolatries which have affected and still affect the contemporary Church with its reliance upon what Turner calls an 'ideological instinct to stabilize the universe upon absolute sources and referents of meaning, upon idolatrous myths, whether of God or of the human', and to return, joyfully, to the earlier ways described by Helen Waddell where 'starlit darkness' can replace the 'queen light' of the recent past. Why this is so is difficult to say. Perhaps it is the eventual realization that the last century has seen so much horror and death that at last our confidence in 'queen light' has expired. Perhaps we have realized that over-reliance upon 'queen light' has actually caused the horror we have experienced. Perhaps the Holocaust has jolted our collective consciousness, for certainly some of those who write in this vein now are heirs to that burning. But whatever the causes, the way is now clear. The only question will be whether the contemporary Church will take it.

9

The Affirmative Way

All mysticism, whether affirmative or negative, whether concerned with speech or silence, knowing or unknowing, is essentially doxological. It is at root a hymn to the existence and nature of God, an intuition and a celebration of God's being. Whether affirmative or negative in its expression, mysticism is that way of talking about God which intuits, affirms and celebrates his nature as it is revealed in his movement towards us in creation. It is a hymn to his hidden presence among us, a song of his deep desire to draw us into himself and our profound yearning for him. It is a hymn of his spokenness as he speaks his nature into existence through his Word, Jesus Christ.

But understanding mysticism in this way requires a prior understanding of the creation as itself being an expression of the being of God. This contrasts sharply with much popular under- standing which is anaemic and weak by comparison because it has been under the thrall of a Newtonian and static view of a universe controlled by little more than a number of scientifically observable and immutable laws. Consequently we have come to understand the doctrine of creation to be some sort of religious attempt to explain how that sort of world came into existence. Our contemporary doctrine of creation then becomes no more than a religious response to the scientific accounts of the evolution of the universe. Christianity now desperately needs to recover a sense of creation as being far more than some sort of back-footed response to scientific claims, a reactive attempt to show that God is, after all, the first cause. When it does then it will be released into a deeper and richer understanding of the mystical way.

The doctrine of creation is primarily an affirmation that all being is from God. Thomas Merton makes this point when he says that the doctrine of creation starts not from a question about being but from a direct intuition of the act of being:

> For God is present to me in the very act of my own being, an act which proceeds directly from His will and is His gift. My act of being is a direct participation in the Being of God. God is pure Being, this is to say He is the pure and infinite Act of total Reality. All other realities are simply reflections of His pure Act of Being, and participations in it granted by His free gift.[1]

This contemplative or mystical way of understanding creation has been obscured to us, but now, in the early twenty-first century, as we slowly face the breakdown of the Newtonian view, we can recover our sense of participation in the divine and we are able to recover an understanding of the creation as an outpouring of Being. The growth of our knowledge of the changing patterns of the universe will enable us to see it as an outpouring, an overwhelming and constant excess of striving and desirous energy, a creativity which will not, indeed, by all the evidence, cannot stop happening, and in which constant new forms, new levels of complexity are always being revealed. In short, the new science reveals the universe as a passion, an expression of the need to love and to have something to love which comes from the aching and overwhelming *passio* at the heart of God.

It is precisely this outpouring of the creation which is at the heart of the mystical life. The mystic intuits the very essence of God as being a *passio*, a heart-aching outpouring which cannot be quenched. Pseudo-Dionysius talks of God as ecstasy. God is the one who cannot help but stand outside of himself in his essential activity, who cannot remain at home but who is also always within himself. In one place Dionysius speaks of God as suffering from some sort of divine inebriation in which he, like a drunken lover, 'Stands outside of all good things, being the superfullness of all these things'.[2] Elsewhere he says, 'It must be said that the very cause of the universe in the beautiful, good superabundance of his benign yearning for all is carried outside of himself in the loving care he has for everything.'[3]

But it is not just Pseudo-Dionysius who speaks in these terms. Eckhart, centuries later, speaks of God as having some sort of overabundance to his nature, what he calls an 'ebullitio', a boiling over. He talks of God's life as springing up and then boiling over into creation. In his commentary on Exodus, Eckhart says, when talking about the words of God 'I am who I am' (Exodus 3.14), that the prior ground of creation is the emanation of the persons of the Godhead; he reflects that the very phrase 'I am who I am'

> indicates a 'boiling' or giving birth to itself – glowing in itself and melting and boiling in and into itself. ... Therefore John 1 says, 'In him was life' (Jn 1.4). 'Life' expresses a type of pushing out by which something swells up in itself and first breaks out totally in itself, each part into each part, before it pours itself forth and 'boils over' on the outside.[4]

Eckhart also often uses the imagery of the well-spring: 'I sometimes mention two springs. One spring from which grace gushes forth, is where the Father begets His only begotten Son ... Another spring is where creatures flow out of God.'

It is important for us to understand that much of this stems from the way in which the mystics of this period are far more comfortable than we moderns are with the idea that God is *eros*, erotic love. For them the very nature of God is expressed by this word. Eros is a force, the force or drive which animates all things and which comes from God. It is always at work and we cannot avoid it. What happens, according to the medieval writers, is that we misuse or misdirect what is actually given us by God, but this force of yearning, this power of love which constantly wills unity and draws us to God, is what energizes the whole of creation. The word for this force is Eros. It is the yearning, desirous, ecstatic outpouring of love which, for the medieval mystic, characterizes God. By contrast we have inherited a suspicion that Eros, erotic love, is earthly and therefore unsuitable for expressing the nature of God. This is compounded by the fact that we have also inherited, from a number of theologians in the nineteenth and twentieth centuries, the view that the New Testament uses the Greek word *agape* rather than *eros* to express the essential nature of God. Agape is, we are told, the word for active love, the love that does good deeds. By using this word as determinative of the nature of God we have slipped into the view that God and the world we inhabit are somehow separate, and the world is the place where God has to go in order to correct its faults, rather like a kindly person exercising agape towards the sick and the wounded. In one sense there is nothing wrong with this, but an understanding of it as central and normative makes it difficult to think or speak in the same terms as the mystics use. If we are to understand them then we have to overcome this prejudice. Moreover, if we are to understand the affirmative way, the way of talking about God which involves the outpouring of metaphor after metaphor in order to catch something of the ecstasy of God in creating and redeeming the world, then we have to employ a richer and deeper basic category than simple *agape* can provide. Moreover we shall, if we are not careful, find ourselves outpaced, as indeed the Church has been, and find ourselves in a situation where the erotic is enshrined in secular literature while theology is left with meagre categories of action and moralization. This will ensure that the Church is increasingly marginalized and has little or nothing to do with a – if not the – major preoccupation of the so-called secular world. We will have banished the erotic into the secular and thereby curtailed our capacity to speak with and for the world which we inhabit.

The tradition, even the earliest theological tradition of the Church, does not make the same mistake. We only have to look, for example, at the work of the earliest Fathers to realize that they were not as circumscribed as we have become in their understanding of God. If we look at the work of Origen, one of the primary influences on the earliest theological traditions, we shall see that he did not suffer, as many twentieth-century Christians have done, from a need to distinguish between love as agape and love as eros, suffering from the misapprehension that eros is sexual and human while agape is active and godlike. For him God was eros, the God who chooses to go out of himself in creation so that he can say, 'I do not think one could be blamed if one called God Passionate Love, just as John calls him Charity.'[5]

Origen writes at the point of crossroads between Greek and Christian thinking. He is concerned to bring biblical categories to bear upon the philosophy of his day. God is no impassible, unchangeable, ultimate principle, but the one who asserts his essential creativity in speaking the word in creation with such passion that there is a kind of 'suffering' in God as he pours himself out as the incarnate Word. He is the one who loves his creation by pouring himself out in agonized devotion. And if there is any suspicion that this is an intellectualized picture then Origen calls up the witness of the New Testament texts, particularly those found in St John, to show that this erotic love was at work in Christ the Word of God. Moreover, if God is eros then the human task is to return by eros to God. The inner person has been created in God's image and must direct the inner erotic longing of the soul back to the one from whom it came. This longing can, of course, be misdirected, but its ultimate purpose is clear. So the soul and God are subject to a mutual erotic longing which (at least as far as Origen was concerned) is not sexual, not simply to do with the joining of bodies, but is a deeply passionate desire for unity.

Once that is understood then several things fall into place. First, it becomes clear that if the creation is an outpouring of the ecstatic love of God then it is ultimately all an expression of God. It is not just sacred because God made it, or because we are asked to be stewards of it, it is all and always part of God's self-expression. As Merton says, 'All being is from God'. So the creation is glory, it is the glory that both covers and reveals God's presence. The creation is the 'Shekinah', the covering of the Lord among us. It also becomes clear why the medievals favoured certain scriptural texts which, for them, showed the erotic force of the presence of God among us. Genesis and the Psalms are eternal favourites, along with St John's Gospel and the Book of Exodus – all of which speak of the presence of the Lord, the Word of creation being poured out in creation and redemption. Above all it becomes clear why the Song of Songs becomes the scriptural text which, once its true spiritual meaning has been discerned, contains the central message of the scriptures as a whole. Origen's exposition of the Song of Songs stands at the beginning of fifteen hundred years of Christian commentary upon this one book as the ultimate parable of the love of God for the soul. So Origen and those who follow him understand the opening verse of the Song, with its famous phrase 'Let him kiss me with the kisses of his mouth!', to be a metaphor for the reception of the Word and its teaching by the human soul. The kiss is the Word coming to its own for which it has longed. 'When her mind is filled with divine perception and understanding without the agency of human or angelic ministration, then she may believe that she has received the kisses of the Word of God himself.'[6]

Similar interpretations are given to the other erotic images contained in the Song of Songs. The 'breasts which are better than wine' refer to the inner ground of the heart of Christ upon which the beloved disciple reposed at the last supper. The treasures which the soul receives from Christ's breast are better than the wine of the law

and the prophets. The references to 'the wound of love' in the Song
are taken to refer to the Word which is the arrow or dart of the
Father whose love strikes and wounds the soul. What is undeniable
is the intensity of the imagery which reflects the intensity of the love
which the Father has for his creation and the corresponding intensity
of the longing which the soul has for God. There is a deep sharpness,
indeed a passionate urgency about the whole matter which is derived
from the intensity of Origen's theological vision of God as eros and
which, consequently, only the power of human eroticism as
expressed in the Song of Songs has the imagery to convey.

So perhaps one of the greatest losses that nineteenth and
twentieth-century theology has suffered has been its inability to
comment upon this book. As almost no other book of the Bible apart
from Genesis or the Psalms, this was the touchstone for medieval
commentary from Origen to St John of the Cross. For more than a
thousand years it was the representative text. It spoke so clearly of
the quest of God for fulfilment, and embodied in such powerful and
immediate language the good news of God's longing for the soul
and the longing of the soul for God, that it was understood as the text
in which all of the gospel could be found. Even when the Christian
tradition abandoned exposition of this book and writers on
mysticism such as Dean Inge in the nineteenth century derided its
influence as 'simply deplorable', it has continued to fascinate the
western imagination. Jungians cannot leave it alone, it appears
briefly in Tennyson and Dorothy Sayers and then, frequently and
terribly, in the poetry of Paul Celan. Now, thankfully, it is gradually
making its return and feminist biblical commentators, sensing its
lack in our male-oriented interpretative world and the capacity the
text has to undermine male-dominated expressions of power and
love, have turned to the text to enable us to retrieve a better world.[7]

All of that is fine and true, but the more important reason why our
unwillingness to comment upon it has been a loss to the theological
history of the nineteenth and twentieth centuries is because such
non-use reveals that we are afraid or unable to allow the beauty and
power of human sexuality in the world to be a metaphor for the
beauty and power of God in his longing for humanity. Eros has been
displaced and our doctrine of the creation diminished. The
nineteenth and twentieth centuries might well have understood
God to be the source of beauty, the creation might well have been
understood to be a reflection of God's infinite imagination, but none

of those understandings carry much hint of the sharp, dark intensity of God's need for us or that of the creation for him that is conveyed by the erotic longings expressed in the Song of Songs. The recovery of a capacity by the Church to use imagery such as that contained in the Song will be part and parcel of a recovery by the Church of the 'erotic' understanding of the creation which haunted the first thousand years of the Christian faith. It will also be the means by which the Church will recover from the colour blindness from which it has suffered over the last two centuries and will be able to relate more directly to the ultimate concerns of the world in which we live. Simone Weil comments: 'To reproach mystics with loving God by means of the faculty of sexual love is as though one were to reproach a painter with making pictures by means of colours composed of material substances.'[8]

Of course, the greatest exponent of the Song of Songs was Bernard of Clairvaux. In his great sequence of sermons on the Song, Bernard sees the Word of God as the medicine of the soul, penetrating us, calling us to lift up our faces and to look upon the most serene face of the Bridegroom. When that happens we shall receive the kisses of his mouth. Bernard frequently uses the famous image of the three kisses: the kiss of the feet in penitence, the kiss of the hand for encouragement and the kiss of the lips for the full joy of the Lord's presence among us. As Turner says, 'Bernard is in love with God erotically'.[9] He uses the language of the medieval tradition to show how the soul can be united with the outpouring of the love of God. God is eros and we respond to him by means of eros already implanted in our soul. His image has been implanted in us and provides us, since it is an energy, not just a form, with the means by which we may find our way back to him.

The love of God is the very centre of Bernard's mysticism, and there are, as is well known, stages in the soul's ascent to God. In his treatise *On Loving God*, Bernard says that we move from carnal love, 'by which a person loves himself for his own sake before everything', to loving God for the sake of what God has done for us, and then to loving God for God's sake. There is a final, fourth stage, which is hardly obtainable in this life, in which we love ourselves but only for God's sake. This emphasis on the different degrees of ascent to God, a characteristic of almost all the mystical writings of this period, only demonstrates how much the love of God is a divine attraction, a force which draws us closer and closer to its origin in

God, who is himself not conscious of loving, not a being who as it were oversees and owns his loving, but is all love, nothing else but love. This love has a power and vehemence which captures the heart and calls for a similar impetuosity in return. In one of the sermons on the Song of Songs Bernard comments on the phrase in the Song 'Have you seen him whom my soul loves?':

> O headlong love, vehement, burning, impetuous, which cannot think of anything besides yourself! You feel distaste for other things, condemning everything besides yourself in self-absorption. You mix up proper order, you leave ordinary usage unnoticed, you are ignorant of due measure.[10]

This is the impetuous, yearning, vehement love which is God, and which is placed in us as the means by which we may return to God. For Bernard the purpose of the religious life is to provide the context within which this very force, this eros, can be channelled, ordered and given the chance to flourish in its proper and fullest fashion, rather than being wasted and misdirected in selfishness. Religion for him was not so much an appropriation of a teaching as an involvement in a passion.

It would, of course, be untrue to say that this affective tradition, with its emphasis on the erotic longing of the soul for God, died out at the end of the Middle Ages. St John of the Cross, as we shall see, uses it in the sixteenth century, but this time in its negative rather than its affirmative form. But historically speaking we do have to wait until the seventeenth century when Traherne resurrects the tradition in England in an expression of the affirmative way to God which includes all of the same eroticism of St Bernard. It is difficult to ascertain how or why Traherne came to the views that he did at this particular juncture in English history. Perhaps it was the influence of the Cambridge Platonists – there is some evidence that through them he knew the work of Gregory of Nazianzus; perhaps it was his love of the beauty of the countryside – that certainly worked its power on him at one important stage in his life; perhaps it was his patent love of the scriptures. But however it came about Traherne sees the world as an expression of the love of God which is invisibly at work in us and all things. This love he calls desire or 'wanting':

For giving me desire,
An eager thirst, a burning, ardent fire,
A virgin, infant flame,
A love with which into the world I came,
An inward, hidden, heavenly love
which in my soul did work and move
And ever, ever me inflame
With restless longing, heavenly avarice
That never could be satisfied,
That did incessantly a paradise
Unknown suggest, and some thing undescried
Discern, and bear me to it; be
Thy name forever praised by me.[11]

What eros was to the medievals, desire or wanting is to Traherne. He explains that God wants and that wanting is a sort of eternal fountain within him. We find this in a section of *Centuries of Meditations* which links Traherne directly with the mystics of the Middle Ages and the Dionysian tradition, a section in which the imagery directly recalls so much we have already found in Origen, Eckhart and Bernard.

> This is very strange that God should want. For in him is the fulness of all Blessedness: He overfloweth eternally. His wants are as glorious as infinite: perfective needs that are in His nature, and ever Blessed because always satisfied. He is from all eternity full of want, or else He would not be full of Treasure. Infinite want is the very ground and cause of infinite treasure. It is incredible yet very plain. Want is the fountain of all His fulness. Want in God is treasure to us. For had there been no need He would not have created the World, nor made us, nor manifested His wisdom, nor exercised His power, nor beautified Eternity, nor prepared the Joys of Heaven. But he wanted Angels and Men, Images, Companions: and these He had from all eternity.[12]

Having affirmed that the very nature of God is wanting, he then goes on in a series of passages to affirm that the human calling is to respond to the 'wanting' of God by a similar reciprocal 'wanting' which will then return us to the blessedness we have lost:

> You must want like a God that you may be satisfied like God. Were you not made in his Image? ... Be present with your want

of a Deity, and you shall be present with the Deity. You shall adore and admire him, enjoy and prize him; believe in Him and Delight in Him, see him to be the fountain of all your joys, and the Head of all your treasures.[13]

Like St Bernard (and Origen before him) Traherne is sure that so many on this earth, although made in God's image, fritter this treasure away in misdirected living. The key to renewal of life is to see where all of your desires come from and to redirect them to their origin so that you can then participate in the end for which you were destined from the beginning.

The central point of this 'return' is found in the cross of Christ, that point of agony where the agony of God in love for the world can meet the agony of humanity in reaching for a return to its source. A careful reading of the 'First Century' shows that Traherne's understanding of the cross, said by some to be inadequate or defective, is absolutely central to his picture and perfectly in tune with orthodox understanding. The cross is the point through which humanity is drawn in to God. Here we can be drawn away from that aimless loitering which is the fate of so many, drawn from an undirected or misdirected life into God. The cross is the point at which we are drawn, lifted up, into the presence of God by the power of divine attraction; it is the point at which our wanting is returned to its source, where our desire is melded with the desire of God, where humanity is broken only to be broken open to new life. Philip Sheldrake comments on this in his essay on the place of desire in the spiritual life:

The passion of Jesus is not simply God's reaction to the fallen condition of humanity. Neither incarnation nor redemption is, strictly speaking, forced upon God. Our own experience is that to long for something is to anguish and at times to suffer spiritual pain. Equally there is an inherent connection between God's eternal longing and the agony of suffering for the loved one that is expressed in the cross of Jesus.[14]

This, then, is the source of what has superficially been called Traherne's 'nature mysticism'. He is not, strictly speaking, a nature mystic, nearer to pagan mythology than to Christian, the property of Greens and Neo-Celtic Revivalism. He is the property of the orthodox Christian mystical tradition in direct line with Pseudo-Dionysius, Eckhart and Julian of Norwich, a tradition in which the normative understanding of the love of God is expressed by the word eros and all that eros involves. He is an outcrop of this tradition at a point of history when one least expected it, when it appeared to have gone underground under the influence of the Puritan movement. He is a sign of truth at the point when the bells of the Restoration rang out once more across the English countryside, when religious and learned men and women together once again took an interest in the mystery of the creation, a sign that the erotic was still present in English theology. For Traherne the countryside is so glorious, the creation itself so wonderful not because it is pretty or even because humanity is called to care for it, but because it is a direct outpouring of the wanting of God. It is part of the over-flowing, the 'ebullitio' of which Eckhart spoke; it is a manifestation of the glory of God, the true Shekinah. Men and women are themselves part of that wanting and that Shekinah but can only live as such when they allow that wanting in them to return to its source. In that famous passage in the 'Third Century' when Traherne recognizes that 'The corn was orient and immortal wheat, which never should be reaped, nor was ever sown',[15] the key sentences are those which are redolent of so much of the earlier tradition: 'Eternity was manifest in the light of the Day, and something infinite behind everything appeared; *which talked with my expectation and moved my desire*' (my italics). That 'something' is the yearning of God which talks to the human yearning and calls it out, lifts it into the life of God from which it came and for which it was made.

It might be thought that, with the demise of Traherne, an understanding of God as eros had once again disappeared were it not for a number of recent developments in our way of looking at the created universe which release our capacity to speak in these ways again. The most important thing that has happened is that the old scientism has died. We are in a scientifically postmodern situation. We no longer see the universe in terms of strict cause and effect, governed by immutable 'laws of nature'. The whole universe is far more complex than we had believed, with different ways of understanding it being found to be appropriate at different times and at different levels of investigation. Unfortunately many in the Church see this as no more than an increased threat. Scientific developments in the study of creation having once frightened us back into a static doctrine of creation, further developments only seem to redouble that fear. However, one or two contemporary

theologians have had the courage and the imagination to see things
in a different light. They wish to take on board the developments of
contemporary scientific enquiry, both in the physical and in the
biological sciences. With the aid of a more dynamic theology, a
more 'erotic' model of understanding, they are able to rediscover the
universe as a complex and multi-layered expression of the erotic
longing of God. Sara Maitland, for example, believes that the most
recent developments in science should not be seen as a threat to
theology but as an opportunity to enlarge our view of God. She says:

> scientists, far from pushing us into an apologetic God-of-the-Gaps
> sheepishness, are in fact opening up for us a vision of God
> infinitely greater, bigger, cleverer, wilder than our somewhat
> stunted imaginations have allowed us; a God who is not tamed
> and constructed by our definitions; a God who challenges us.[16]

What she is reaching after is a view of God as the erotic drunken
lover that the medieval mystics held but were not able to explore in
the same way simply because they were not familiar with post-
Einsteinian physics or contemporary discoveries in biology. Somebody who is familiar with those developments and who does have
the courage to begin to relate them to an earlier theological tradition
is the American writer and theologian Annie Dillard. She, as a
young biologist, decided to take a break and live alone for a year,
Thoreau-like, in the Appalachian mountains. The diary of her year's
retreat, *Pilgrim at Tinker Creek*, records her reactions and her
endeavour to link her biological insights with the earlier Christian
tradition.

As she walks about the land around her house and reads about
what she finds, Dillard is amazed at the complexity, variety and
horror of the universe in which she lives. She writes in wonder and
sometimes in rage at the complexity and conflict and beauty and
sheer dazzling colour of what she sees and what she discovers; but
then, quietly, in the interstices of her wonder, inserts some insights
that show that it is we who need to find a new view of the creator, or,
perhaps, re-find an older view of the creator that we have lost. She
points out that many of us are still living in the world of Newtonian
physics but that Heisenberg with his Principle of Indeterminacy has
pulled the rug from under our feet. Scientists might then feel, as one
of them said, that such a move now leaves us with no clear distinction between the natural and the supernatural. 'These physicists',

she says, 'are again mystics, as Kepler was, standing on a rarefied mountain pass, gazing transfixed into an abyss of freedom.'[17]

At another point, Dillard reflects that we have to learn again to see. She recounts what happens to people who have been long blind but who have had their sight restored. They see for the first time and often find the experience disorienting; they keep their eyes closed because they are overwhelmed by the vividness of what they see. She is reminded of a Hasidic tale told by Martin Buber:

> Rabbi Mendel once boasted to his teacher Rabbi Elimelekh that evenings he saw the angel who rolls away the light before the darkness, and mornings the angel who rolls away the darkness before the light. 'Yes,' said Rabbi Elimelekh, 'in my youth I saw that too. Later on you don't see these things any more.'[18]

Annie Dillard comments:

> Why didn't someone hand those newly sighted people paints and brushes from the start, when they still didn't know what anything was? Then maybe we all could see color-patches too, the world unraveled from reason, Eden before Adam gave names. The scales would drop from my eyes; I'd see trees like men walking; I'd run down the road against all orders, hallooing and leaping.[19]

At the end of her meditation she launches into a paean of praise and thanksgiving for the secret divinity which inhabits the universe. This divinity, she hints, is not 'nice' in the way that we would like it to be, for it sets the universe free to be and we are not spared death or disaster. All of our needs are met and everything is given to us, but not as the world gives. We will not keep anything we love, but our needs will all be met.

> I think that the dying pray at the last not 'please,' but 'thank you,' as a guest thanks his host at the door. ... Divinity is not playful. The universe was not made in jest but in solemn incomprehensible earnest. By a power that is unfathomably secret, and holy, and fleet. There is nothing to be done about it, but ignore it, or see. And then you walk fearlessly ...[20]

Annie Dillard has seen, through the maze of modern biological and physical knowledge, something of the erotic earnest with which the world was created. She says:

Intricacy is that which is given from the beginning, the birthright,
and in intricacy is the hardiness of complexity that ensures against
the failure of all life. ... We walk around; we see a shred of the
infinite possible combinations of an infinite variety of forms.

Anything can happen; any pattern of speckles may appear in a
world ceaselessly bawling with newness....

The wonder is that all the forms are not monsters, that there is
beauty at all, grace gratuitous, pennies found ... Beauty itself is
the fruit of the creator's exuberance that grew such a tangle...

This, then, is the extravagant landscape of the world, given,
given with pizzazz, given in good measure, pressed down, shaken
together, and running over.[21]

And so the affirmative way comes alive again in the contemporary
world as and when we allow ourselves, as Annie Dillard says, to see
the world 'unraveled from reason'. Then we will see it as it is, and
in union with Julian of Norwich say, 'See, I am God: see, I am in all
things: see, I never lift my hands off my works, nor ever shall,
without end ... How should anything be amiss?' The affirmative
mystic is not simply someone who believes that the created world is
beautiful or reflects the beauty of a God who is distant and who has
left this beauty in the care of humankind. He or she is one who
affirms, from a movement of their own being, that the universe is
itself an expression of the exuberance and passion of an 'erotic'
God, that human beings themselves are created with the same
exuberance and passion within them so that they can, by a
movement of that passion, know the reality of God for themselves.
In our own day this has two very important corollaries. The first is
that it should, in a postmodern scientific climate, enable the believer
to understand and to affirm developments in the scientific understanding of the world which at first sight appear to threaten belief in
a creator because they threaten our understanding of order in the
universe. In fact we should now know that it has been our conviction
that the universe is controlled by reason that has been mistaken. The
Church should, perhaps, have resisted this supremacy with greater
imagination and greater courage – certainly with a closer eye to the
theology of the earliest Church. It is now at a distinct disadvantage
as the theologies it has developed have been developed in order to
respond to reason when they should have been developed to enchant
or imagination. When pure reason is not the only category the

scientific community needs all we are able to supply them with are tired ghosts.

The secondary corollary is that this should enable us to understand the centrality that the erotic has for our culture. That this is so is not a sign of depravity, rather a sign that the world somehow knows, perhaps often without really knowing, what the central core of life's energy really is. We do the secular world no service by condemning its preoccupation with the erotic, rather we should learn from it that the erotic is the truth, and in conversation enable the world to discover from whence it comes and to live accordingly. Passion is well known, what appears to be less well known is where it comes from and how it can redeem. St Bernard was right to say that the task of the Church is to enable the world to love properly.

10
The Negative Way

The negative way to God derives from over-saturation by the divine rather than lack of faith or abandonment by God. It is the result of a dazzling by the all-too-present love of God; it is not a sign of our distance from God. It is the point at which our attempts to speak about God break down because we are too close to an overwhelming reality, not the point at which nothing is spoken of because nothing is seen. On the contrary, so much is seen that the eyes have to be shut tight in order to begin to tolerate what is happening. Many of the mystical writers talk about the light of God as being 'a dazzling ray of darkness' in order to convey their meaning. God's proximate presence is, as it were, a lightning flash which suddenly illuminates the darkness and fills the world with a strange brilliance. It is so bright that it immediately plunges everything into a deeper darkness than before, except that the eye is so seared with the brightness that it cannot rid itself of the image that is created within it. St John of the Cross speaks of the dark night as

> an inflow of God into the soul that purges it of its habitual ignorances and imperfections. ... Yet a doubt arises: Why, if it is a divine light (for it illumines souls and purges them of their ignorances), does one call it a dark night? ... The brighter the light the more the owl is blinded; and the more one looks at the brilliant sun, the more the sun darkens the faculty of sight. ... This is why St Dionysius and other mystical theologians call this infused contemplation a ray of darkness.[1]

Understanding the so-called 'negative way' or what has become known as 'the dark night of the soul' in this manner enables us to see its intrinsic relationship with the affirmative way. They are both results of understanding God as Eros. All mysticism, whether affirmative or negative, is thus a response to the plenitude of God, a way of speaking about his self-outpouring. All mysticism is thus also an involvement in the actual nature of God, not simply a set of reflections about him or a series of interesting analogies of his presence or absence in the universe. Above all, *negative* mysticism is not a way of talking about God's literal absence; it is, rather, a profound way of talking about his overwhelming presence and the essential difference that makes to human beings when once they have decided to acknowledge it. It is therefore, properly speaking, incorrect to attempt to use the negative way, or the metaphor of the dark night of the soul, as a means of talking about the loss of faith in the twentieth century, or indeed the loss of faith at any time. This strand in Christianity cannot be equated with, used as a metaphor for, or even provide a justification for literal loss of faith. As we have seen, there are certainly parallels between the negative way and a number of twentieth-century religious phenomena, such as the sense of absence spoken of by faithful Christians who are troubled by the overwhelming and exclusive use of a terminology of light as a means of describing God or Christ, and there are parallels between the negative way and the experience of depression in certain circumstances. But ultimately the negative way arose as a way of expressing belief, not as a way of talking about unbelief. Moreover, to understand it as resulting from an *excess* of light allows the contemporary Church to retrieve its proper use in contemporary self-expression rather than simply understanding the negative way as a historical phenomenon of no real use to people in the modern world.

Ultimately negative mysticism speaks of the interior chambers of the human spirit, of their original emptiness and of the need for them to remain empty in order properly to receive and be filled with the Bridegroom. Negative mysticism speaks of the essentially incomplete nature of the human self and the necessity for those who believe to accept that incompleteness in order to be filled with God. In this way, as we shall see, negative mysticism provides a powerful critique of modernism and the so-called fulfilment modernism offers. Negative mysticism is also an eschatological metaphor for the spiritual life, the proper means of speaking about the constant, dark longing of faith, what Gregory of Nyssa called *epektasis*, the 'how long, O Lord, how long?' of the psalmist, and regarded by Gregory and others as one of the essential characteristics of the Christian vocation.

In the earliest years of the Christian faith the quintessential mystic was not one who found themself united with God in some sort of ineffable, unitive experience, the one who, as it were, hugged God to the chest so tight that they were one in essence, but rather the one who had to endure an overwhelming darkness, even at the mountain top. For all the early Christian writers the 'type' of the mystic was Moses, who had climbed up the mountain after a long instruction in the faith but even there could only hide in the cleft in the rocks while the Lord passed by and had to accept that all he would be allowed to see would be the 'back parts' of God. For the Fathers of the Church the key text was found in Exodus where Moses asks to see the glory of God. God replies that he will make all of his goodness pass before Moses and that he will show mercy on whom he will show mercy:

'But ... you cannot see my face; for no one shall see me and live.' And the Lord continued, 'See, there is a place by me where you shall stand on the rock; and while my glory passes by I will put you in a cleft of the rock, and I will cover you with my hand until I have passed by; then I will take away my hand, and you shall see my back; but my face shall not be seen.'[12]

Gregory of Nyssa, commenting, says:

The munificence of God assented to the fulfilment of his desire, but did not promise any cessation of satiety of the desire. He would not have shown himself to his servant if the sight were such as to bring the desire of the beholder to an end, since the true sight of God consists in this, that the one who looks up to God never ceases in that desire. For he says: *You cannot see my face, for man cannot see me and live.* Scripture does not indicate that this causes the death of those who look, for how would the face of life ever be the cause of death to those who approach it? On the contrary, the Divine is by its nature life giving. Yet the characteristic of the divine nature is to transcend all characteristics. Therefore, he who thinks God is something to be known does not have life, because he has turned away from true Being to what he considers by sense perception to have being.[3]

This is a crucial text for the understanding of the negative way and its origins in Christian history for it makes clear that God is life and that all mysticism, of whatever kind, even negative speech about God, stems from a proper sense of God's fullness. It also makes clear God's difference, the fact that she transcends all 'characteristics', for God is not like human beings and cannot be recognized as having human characteristics. So the possession of God by human beings is an impossibility and if we think we 'have' or 'know' God directly then that is a certain indication that we do not. All of these themes, stated here by Gregory very early on in the Christian tradition, appear in different ways right through the apophatic literature until John of the Cross in the sixteenth century, and represent a critique of much modern theology.

Gregory enlarges upon this in his comments on Exodus 20.21 when he speaks of the darkness of God: 'Then the people stood at a distance, while Moses drew near to the thick darkness where God was.' He continues:

> For leaving behind everything that is observed, not only what sense comprehends but also what the intelligence thinks it sees, it keeps on penetrating deeper until by the intelligence's yearning for understanding it gains access to the invisible and the incomprehensible, and there it sees God. This is the true knowledge of what is sought; this is the seeing that consists in not seeing, because that which is sought transcends all knowledge, being separated on all sides by incomprehensibility as by a kind of darkness. Wherefore John the sublime, who penetrated into the luminous darkness, says, *No one has ever seen God*, thus asserting that knowledge of the divine essence is unattainable not only by men but also by every intelligent creature.[4]

Gregory of Nyssa wrote during the springtime of the Christian Church in the fourth century. Pseudo-Dionysius systematized this thinking in Syria in the early sixth century, but the tradition lived on through the vicissitudes of the development of the faith and blossomed in Europe in the Middle Ages. Meister Eckhart quotes Dionysius, but the writer most under his spell, or at least what he assumed was his spell, but in reality filtered through the work of many others, especially Thomas Gallus, was the author of *The Cloud of Unknowing*, that gem of English mystical theology of the fourteenth century. For the author of this manual of prayer desire for God is central to the human person and God is known not by the intelligence but by love, when the desire of love meets the grace of God in an impulse of love which reaches into the cloud of unknowing. The author says:

our Lord has, in his great mercy, called you and led you to him by the desire of your heart....[5]

Do not hang back then, but labour in it until you experience the desire. For when you first begin to undertake it, all that you find is a darkness, a sort of cloud of unknowing; you cannot tell what it is, except that you experience in your will a simple reaching out to God. This darkness and cloud is always between you and your God, no matter what you do, and it prevents you from seeing him clearly by the light of understanding in your reason ... So set yourself to rest in this darkness as long as you can, always crying out after him whom you love.[6]

 This desire is placed in us by the source of desire and is described in a very vivid phrase as 'a leash of longing': 'And so with his great grace he kindled your desire, and fastened to it a leash of longing, and with this led you into a more special state and degree of life.'[7]

Similarly, St John of the Cross, two hundred years later, when speaking of the dialogue between the bride and the bridegroom in *The Spiritual Canticle*, uses the phrase 'love stirring breezes', which he likens to the 'still small voice' heard by Elijah at the mouth of the cave in Horeb (1 Kings 19.11–13). St John of the Cross comments:

Since this touch of God gives intense satisfaction and enjoyment to the substance of the soul, and gently fulfils her desire for this union, she calls this union, or these touches, love stirring breezes. ... She calls the knowledge a whistling, because just as the whistling of the breeze pierces deeply into the hearing organ, so this most subtle and delicate knowledge penetrates into the innermost part of the substance of the soul, and the delight is greater than all other.[8]

But John goes on to say that this 'most subtle and delicate knowledge' is 'not clear, but dark':

'for it is contemplation, which in this life, as St Dionysius says, is a ray of darkness. We can say that it is a ray and image of fruition, since fruition takes place in the intellect. This substance that is understood, and which the soul calls whistling, is equivalent to 'the eyes I have desired' of which the soul said, when they were being revealed to her, 'Withdraw them beloved,' because her senses could not endure them.[9]

Citing these writers at length enables us to see how the dark way to God is not a result of a sense of absence but of a superfluity of presence; how the mystical tradition believed that the intelligence could not attain God, thus confirming Aquinas' insight many years later that we cannot know what God is like; and how 'darkness' in God is really a sort of seeing which is a not seeing, a breakdown, if you like, of the capacity to talk about what 'seeing God' really meant. It was, as the author of *The Cloud* says, not 'a darkness such as you have in your house at night, when your candle is out', but, 'When I say "darkness," I mean a privation of knowing'.[10] It was an overwhelming of the senses by the intensity of the proximity of God.

Nor should anybody think that any of these writers believed that the mystic, whoever he or she might be, reached the mountain top and the darkness of God by any special or private and individualist route. It is not the flight of the alone to the alone. Gregory makes it clear that Moses, the quintessential mystical figure, reached this place only after following the normal ways of Christian development. Gregory's exposition of the incidents in Moses' life before this point are all examples, 'types' or allegories of the normal way of Christian discipleship. The leaving of Egypt is the leaving of sin; the crossing of the Red Sea and the eating of the manna point to the Christian sacraments, and so on. The point is that Moses is the one who has already been through these mysteries and so he enters into the darkness of God not by means of any psychological or intellectual immediacy but because he is a pilgrim being redeemed within the liturgical community of the faithful. The mystical tradition has been severely criticized – and indeed often still is – by those who believe that the mystical writers are more Platonist than Christian and hence have little sense of the need for redemption within the traditional ecclesial and liturgical patterns. Such criticism has been levelled at Pseudo-Dionysius in particular and so, by extension, those whom he influenced. More recent scholarship is, however, quite clear that while Neoplatonic categories of thought are widely used by the early mystical writers, all their writing must be set within the liturgical and sacramental life of the ecclesial community. Andrew Louth is particularly clear about this. Andrew Louth is one of a group of modern scholars who have become convinced that the negative way is not simply a Neoplatonist and therefore heterodox form of Christianity, but can be clearly distinguished from Neoplatonism itself and must be set strictly within the liturgical context of the Church. He says: 'Christian theology, and in particular Christian mystical theology, is ecclesial, it is the fruit of participation in the mystery of Christ, which is inseparable from the mystery of the Church.'[11]

Bernard McGinn, in his study of Dionysius, makes the very same point: 'At the start we must emphasise once again the fundamentally ecclesial and liturgical nature of Dionysian mysticism. . . . Dionysius would claim that to be a true theologian is to pray liturgically.'[12] He cites von Balthasar, who says, 'The whole theology of the Areopagite is for him a single, sacred liturgical act.' With those words we are back to the doxological nature of the mystical journey. Indeed the mystics themselves make the very same point. We have already seen how Gregory of Nyssa believed that Moses only reaches the darkness at the mountain top as a result of and on the back of the ongoing process of growth and development within the liturgical community, symbolized for him in the events of the journey out of Egypt and through the wilderness. *The Cloud* author makes the same comment when he says at the beginning of his book that it should not be placed in the hands of anyone who has not already demonstrated that he is a follower of Christ in the active life as well as the contemplative life. 'He will be one who is doing all that he can, and has been, presumably, for a long time past, to fit himself for the contemplative life by the virtues and exercises of the active life. Otherwise this book is not for him.'[13] The theologians of the negative way themselves make it abundantly clear that what they are talking about must be set and will only be found within the ongoing life of the Christian community. It has only been the spectacles we have been wearing, coloured as they have been by the individualism and experientialism of the twentieth century, that have prevented us from understanding this. As we have already seen, the arrival of postmodernism allows us to take those spectacles off, to retrieve the true nature of the mystical life and to return that life to the people.

But there is more to say about the negative way. If it is not a personalized and ineffable experience, what is it? There are two particular characteristics of the negative way, or rather, two particular 'negative' characteristics of the spiritual life which reveal that life to be authentic. They are the breakdown of the capacity to speak about God and the breakdown of a capacity to speak about the self. Professor Turner calls these the apophaticism of language and the apophaticism of the self. Let us deal with them in turn.

As we discovered, the author of *The Cloud of Unknowing* says, 'When I say "darkness", I mean a privation of knowing ...', and contrasts that with the sort of darkness you might find in your own house when your candles go out. He obviously does not mean simply not being able to see, but rather 'being unable to speak about'. St John of the Cross says the same thing in a different way in his diagram which accompanies *The Ascent of Mount Carmel*. In this sketch – which must have been one of many the saint drew to give to friars to carry around with them and which were not all exactly the same – the route up the mountain is marked by 'goods of heaven' and 'goods of earth'. The goods of heaven are glory, joy, knowledge, consolation and rest. The goods of earth are the same except that possessions replace glory; but against each one of them, on either side, John has marked the words 'nor this', and the path ends with the words 'the more I desired to seek (or possess) them, the less I had'. The saint is here pointing to a similar 'privation' or set of privations on the road to God. God is not this, nor this, nor even, it seems, 'neither this nor that'. This is not simply a set of contradictions, meaningful only to those who have gone this way or who have experienced the ineffable, but pointers to the fact that any language which tries to speak about God in some way breaks down and cannot be used. It is almost as if the mystic is saying that God is beyond assertions about her; yes we know that, but she is also beyond denials about her and beyond both assertions and denials. In other words it is not just that he is beyond anything we can say about him but that language actually breaks down in the very act of speaking about God. The words of St John of the Cross, which we quoted earlier, illustrate this: 'It is contemplation, which in this life, as St Dionysius says, is *a ray of darkness.*' A ray of darkness is, of course, a contradiction in terms, but it is by the use of such contradictions that the mystic shows that what he or she wishes to speak about cannot be contained within language. Professor Turner says that the position of the apophatic theologian is

the same as the person who when lost for a word can only say what it is not, with absolutely no prospect of ever finding the right one, the word which will do full justice to the thought. She may

very well be able to judge some candidates to be more adequate
than others, but this cannot be because she knows the *mot juste* as
a standard of comparison.[14]

This is interesting and important. First, apophatic language reminds
us of the inadequacy of all attempts to speak about *God*. It reminds
us that God is not a thing like any other thing. Negative language is
not a description of actual darkness but "a subversion of any
description of God. But, and equally important, apophatic language
reminds us of the inadequacy of *speaking* about God. Apophatic
language is the breakdown of speech in the face of the divine and so
a reminder not just of the inadequacy of language as such, but a
reminder that we cannot restrict our language to any one set of
metaphors as if that set of metaphors were normative and descriptive. We might use a set of metaphors, such as the metaphors
associated with fatherhood and all that implies because the tradition
has given us those metaphors, but we have to remember that they are
no more than that; they are the signs by which we identify ourselves
with each other and connect with the tradition in which we stand;
they are the ciphers, as it were, for saying 'this is Christian
discourse'. But as Professor Turner points out, this does not mean
that we can then go on to say that God is not the sort of being who
can have a body and so God cannot have a gender. That might
mislead us 'into supposing that God is "spiritual" or "disembo-
died"' in some way. It is better, Professor Turner suggests, to
'describe God both as male and female, then we force upon our
materialistic imaginations a concrete sense of the collapse of gender-
language as such'.[15] A retrieval of apophatic language about God
will, therefore, be of assistance to the contemporary Church in its
struggle to find the correct way of talking about God, for it will
remove the debate from the shrill and oppositional into a realization
that *any* language about God is always a failure. The contemporary
debate so far has, it seems, often given the impression that God is the
property of our language, either male or female.

But apophatic language is not just saying something about the
transcendence of God or even about the inability of language to
speak of this transcendent God; it is also saying something about the
human person. There is an interesting set of passages in the work of
that modern apophatic mystic Thomas Merton which makes this
particularly clear. Merton has been talking about the self and the

distinction, frequent in his writings, between the true self and the false self. The false self is the product of ambition and materialism whereas the true self is that which was given us by God. It is our task, Merton avers, to divest ourselves of the false self in order to return to our authentic self and to live truly. But in a series of meditations Merton then makes it clear that even this true self is not ours and is not the subject of our personality. He says this inmost self is beyond any kind of experience which can have 'I' as its subject and in which there is any separate 'self', because at this point lover and beloved are one. Interestingly he then says that it is effectively impossible to step into this state because there is no 'step' to make at this point:

> The next step is not a step. You are not transported from one degree to another. What happens is that the separate entity that is you apparently disappears and nothing seems to be left but a pure freedom indistinguishable from infinite freedom. ... Would you call this experience?[16]

Merton replies to his own question by saying, 'I think you might say that this only becomes an experience in a man's memory. You are not you, you are fruition. If you like, you do not have an experience, you become Experience ...' He then goes on to speak of the way in which the darkness of mysticism is effectively the breakdown of language:

> And here all adjectives fall to pieces. Words become stupid. Everything you say is misleading – unless you list every possible experience and say: 'That is not what it is.' 'That is not what I am talking about. [*Which, as we have already discovered, is exactly what St John of the Cross does in his diagram.*] Metaphor has now become hopeless altogether. Talk about 'darkness' if you must: but the thought of darkness is already too dense and too coarse.[17]

What Merton points to is the fact that at the heart of the apophatic way is an affirmation of the breakdown of the notion of the self. This should not be news to the student of mysticism, especially those who have read Meister Eckhart carefully. Eckhart is the supreme mystic of the unselfing of the self, or to speak more carefully, the mystic of the dismantling of the sense of need for a self of any kind. For this need for a self is precisely that need which prevents the self entering into the nothingness of God. In his German sermons – the least careful of his writings – Eckhart gives voice to this sense of the suspension of human nature and of the need to abandon even any sense of inwardness or possession, even of God, in order for God to be God in them.

Where the Father gives birth to his Son in the innermost ground, there this nature is suspended. ... As truly as the Father in his simple nature gives his Son birth naturally, so truly does he give him birth in the inward part of the spirit, and that is the inner world. Here God's ground is my ground and my ground is God's ground.[18]

Professor Turner comments:

Eckhart's detachment requires the dismantling of every sense of created selfhood in the breakthrough of the soul into its own ground; there, where its character of being a 'something' is lost, it finds its own 'nothingness' in identity with the 'nothingness' of the ground of God.[19]

Of course, such a view represents a protest, at least, or a critique of the modernist spirit of personal fulfilment, and so it is not surprising that during those years when the Church was grappling to come to terms with the modernist spirit, such insights were relatively sparse in mainstream modern theology. Where they went was into the minds and hearts of some few poets and writers who kept the tradition alive, sometimes by dint of circumstance.

It has been suggested that one of these 'secret mystics' was the nineteenth-century American poet Emily Dickinson. Certainly there is something of the apophatic mystic in her poems, particularly those which deal with the absence or removal of the loved one. It is unknown whether this loved one was the Revd Charles Wadsworth or God, or whether Wadsworth's withdrawal left her to face only God. Certainly she dressed as a 'Bride of the Spirit' and her poems speak of the emptiness that many mystics found. The poems also illustrate by their stark simplicity yet intense feeling something of the breakdown of language of which we have been speaking. The opening lines of her poem 'This World is not Conclusion', with its haunting notes of desire and yet ignorance, is certainly perhaps the nearest that this reclusive poet came to expressing – although surrounded by Puritan America – the glory of the apophatic way:

This World is not Conclusion.
A Species stands beyond –
Invisible, as Music –
But positive, as Sound –
It beckons, and it baffles –
Philosophy – don't know –
And through a Riddle, at the last –
Sagacity, must go –[20]

While Emily Dickinson's work contains hints of the apophatic way, perhaps because her situation rendered her ignorant of the writings of Eckhart or St John of the Cross, it surfaces much more clearly in the work of two twentieth-century poets, Paul Celan and R. S. Thomas. R. S. Thomas's apophaticism is now well known in religious circles. He manages to express an absolute sense of absence by means of images which are homely and natural, such as the recurring awareness in his work of the way in which God constantly recedes from us, is always going before us and is out of reach. We arrive at the place where the hare has been resting only to find the hare gone, but the patch still warm, or we are like the migrating birds, flying towards the North Pole while God recedes before us into his fastness until he reaches a place where even though it is night it is still light all night long.

He is that great void
we must enter, calling
to one another on our way
in the direction from which
he blows. What matter
if we should never arrive
to breed or to winter
in the climate of our conception?

Enough we have been given wings
and a needle in the mind
to respond to his bleak north.

There are times even at the Pole
when he, too, pauses in his withdrawal
so that it is light there all night long.[21]

These images, whether consciously or not, certainly employ the same sense of darkness as an excess of light which characterizes the apophatic writers of the past.

David Scott, another contemporary priest-poet, comments that Thomas's poetry was 'detonated' by his experience of serving the dour hill people of Wales in rural parishes.[22] Emily Dickinson may have come near to the negative way through her experience of the absence of a lover who was also God. None of these experiences, however bleak, can approach the horror of the Holocaust which is the spur for the poetry of Paul Celan.

Paul Celan was a German-speaking East European Jew who lost his parents in the Nazi death camps and was himself subject to labour camps and Soviet occupation. For many German-speaking people his poems have become the touchstone of their reaction to the horrors of this period. They are now translated into English and have won recognition as some of the most powerful expressions of feeling in European poetry. What Celan does is to use images and phrases from the Hebrew scriptures to explore something of the horror of the past. Only thus, by employing the most deep-seated and ancient of images, does he find the vocabulary to relate to the unspeakable. For instance, his celebrated poem *Death Fugue* takes imagery from the Song of Songs and weaves that into relationship with Goethe's Marguerite and the scraping of violins as people went to their death in Auschwitz. For Paul Celan there is a silence, an inability to speak, about the Holocaust which for him is married to the inability to speak about God, the God who, perhaps, allowed it. This inability to speak, so common of much Jewish reaction, brings him into touch with both Jewish mysticism and the apophatic Christian tradition. In 1960 Celan received the celebrated Georg Büchner Prize in Germany and wrote an acceptance speech which became a form of a manifesto of his poetic stance. In it he spoke of the 'darkness' or 'obscurity' of poetry and of 'a wholly other' who must be, as it were, broken open or set free by poetry. Shortly after making this speech Celan wrote one of his most mystical poems, *Psalm*:

> No one kneads us again out of earth and clay,
> no one incants our dust.
> No one.
>
> Blessèd art thou, No One.
> In thy sight would

we bloom.
In thy
spite.

A Nothing
we were, are now, and ever
shall be, blooming:
the Nothing –, the
No One's-Rose.

With
our pistil soul-bright,
our stamen heaven-waste,
our corolla red
from the purpleword we sang
over, O over
the thorn.[23]

This poem speaks of the unknown quality of God and, in one breath,
both denies and affirms his existence and his creatorly powers. As
Joseph Felstiner, Celan's biographer, says: 'In this poem the absent
"No One" of the catastrophe masks the unknowable "No One" of
Jewish Mysticism.'[24] And, we could add, of the Christian apophatic
way. But there was more to come, for in May 1961 Celan wrote
another poem with mystical motifs, called *Mandorla*. Once again
this poem, like *Psalm*, combines positive and negative elements with
resonances from the Hebrew scriptures and faint, but faint echoes of
Christian imagery.

In the almond – what stands in the almond?
The Nothing.
In the almond stands Nothing.
There it stands and stands.

In Nothing – who stands there? The King.
There stands the King, the King.
There he stands and stands.

Jewish curls, no gray for you.

And your eye – whereto stands your eye?
Your eye stands opposite the almond.
Your eye, the Nothing it stands opposite.

It stands behind the King.
So it stands and stands.

Human curls, no gray for you.
Empty almond, royal blue.[25]

Celan had already met 'Nothing' in his reading of Heidegger years
before. More recently he had been reading the Jewish writer on
mysticism, Gershem Scholem, and also at this time had been
translating the poems of Emily Dickinson, whose painful and
condensed poetry he found congenial. In *Mandorla* there is plainly a
presence against which the 'you' of the poem stands, even though
this presence is described as 'Nothing'. In Celan's poems the
almond is often a simile for the Jew or Jewishness, and the almond
stands in the Nothing and the Nothing or the King stands in the
almond. It is important to remember, when reading Celan's intense
lines, that the nothingness of annihilation is never far away and there
is within them, as within him, a struggle to bring the annihilation of
the Holocaust into some sort of symbiosis with the annihilation of
the vision of God, a symbiosis which is always hoped for, always
struggled for, but somehow never really achieved. There were
moments in Celan's life when the two might become one, but in the
end, in 1970, like Primo Levi, another Jewish survivor of the
Holocaust, he commited suicide.

David Scott, writing about the poetry of R. S. Thomas, says:

R. S. Thomas has given my generation of clergy the words to
convey how we have felt about an absent God, the struggle with
increasing numbers of disaffected people who have no need of
God and the idols of modern technology. It has been a bleak
picture and we have had to work hard to see, beneath the
bleakness, the bright field, the field where the sun chances to bring
his favours just briefly. The monastic austerity of his life and his
poems has made these brief glimpses of the sun so much more
powerful.[26]

Whereas that might well be true of Thomas it would be difficult to
say the same of Paul Celan, if only because his poetry not only
speaks of the absence of God but of the nothingness of God and of
the annihilation which happens in the presence of God. In that sense
Celan is much closer to Eckhart as far as the Christian tradition is
concerned, and a much more apophatic poet than Thomas. Indeed

Thomas's negativity pales into insignificance besides that of Celan. The importance of these writers, however, whether Jewish or Christian, is that they point to the breakdown not just of language but also of the self and the self's capacity to speak of God in the face of the immensity of the darkness which God is.

Conclusion

Paul Celan's poetry is the ultimate reminder that modernism has come to an end. The Holocaust, which occasioned it, was the final conflagration of reason and ushers in a new period in which either nihilism reigns or new forms of the faith, new ways of being the faith, can be discovered. The burden of this book has been that the Church should respond to this situation by looking not simply to the past but to its very deepest roots and allow the mystical way to be restated and rediscovered. This will require a deeper search into the mystical tradition than has been the case and a deeper readiness to take seriously the claims of postmodernism. These two forces working together can enable the Church to restate its life and to model the way of Christ so that those who are unable to tolerate the current vogue for 'modernization' in the Church will be able to hear a different drum and know that God is still a possibility for them.

The argument is put that such a way forward is 'élitist' and even 'intellectualist', whereas what the Church has been trying to do in the last few decades has been to speak to people in their own language, using simple doctrinal patterns and simple clear statements of the truth. It is said, with some justification, that we live in a secularized culture and that most people are at a very great distance from the Christian verities. Hence we have to re-evangelize using clear patterns and simple arguments. The real answer is that it is just that approach which is 'intellectualist' since it still addresses the mind of the hearer and so rests upon a rationalist anthropology. Such a view also involves what philosophers would call 'a positivism of language' whereby theological language, which should remain analogical and 'slant', becomes direct and descriptive. It also needs to be said that from the time of Constantine there is always the risk, if not the reality, that a union of power and reason will arise, a union in the face of which the only honest recourse is to flee to the desert. I suspect that is in fact what a large number of people actually do when they cease to attend church in any formal sense. They are simply being Desert Fathers of the heart and remaining within themselves, in their 'cells', until the Church disentangles itself from the 'imperium', whether this be the imperium of the state or, more likely, the imperious requirements of positivist doctrinal language and the accompanying imperious belief that we must survive at all costs.

So this book provides an alternative way. The mystical way is presented here in what may seem to be an 'intellectual' package, but when unpacked it will be seen to be precisely a very unintellectual approach in that it places the disappearance of the modernist 'self' into God at the centre. In other words it is a theology of participation in God, and the mystical way is that way which opens the doors towards this participation by the double means of the praise of the heart and the blinding of the eyes with glory.

The reason why this alternative way is so little understood by the contemporary Church is precisely because God is so real and so enormous and so much God that we find ourselves afraid or unable to use language about him properly. The paucity of mystical language in the present-day Church is because we do not take the reality of God seriously enough and have retreated into simplicities and naiveties, what Les Murray would call 'Narrowspeak'.

In fact we treat God so casually in our modernized, sanitized, quick, light-based Church that she becomes a reality very much like any other reality and so we talk about her as if she were simply another thing in existence. In other words, the paucity of mystical language in the Church derives from a reductionist view of God brought upon us by our assimilation to the spirit of the age. Lack of mystical language is a sign that we have no problem with talking about God. But we should have a problem in talking about God. If we do not have a problem in talking about God, then it is difficult to believe that we have actually taken the unreality of God, that is her absolute existence and hence her unknowability in Aquinas' terms, seriously enough. It might even be questioned whether we actually believe in God in real terms even though at one level we protest that we do.

Two things follow. First of all mysticism is really a sort of theological subversion, a critique both of experience of and language about God. Mysticism asserts the primacy of God over both language and experience and effectively says to the Church, 'There is still more to come. Your talk and your claims to experience are, indeed will never be, enough.' In point of fact mysticism is a form of deconstruction, a way of deliberately unravelling the falsities to which devotion and religious practice and religious speech are prone and returning them to their pristine and raw and uncomprehending beginnings. Mysticism is a way of returning us to that 'starlit darkness' of which Helen Waddell spoke in her study of the Desert Fathers, a darkness in which we can really see and which removes us from the delusory qualities of contemporary existence.

Second, this alternative way gives the mystical tradition back to the people of God. It opens a doorway for all of us to recover the totality of the mystical way in our present age. This is because the rediscovery of the mystical tradition in its totality and wholeness, where the twin sisters of the cataphatic and apophatic way, the praise of the heart and the blinding of the eyes, hold hands together, will affirm God as the source of being and not simply as an object of belief. To do this is to readmit the believer to the realm of theology and to reaffirm his or her capacity for mystical participation in the life of God. It thereby removes the believer from the tyranny of the grand narratives of the past, a tyranny to which he or she has been subject since at least the seventeenth century if not from the time of Constantine. The believer is then able to recover confidence in belief without assuming that a rational acceptance of certain doctrinal statements is a *sine qua non* of participation in the life of the Church. This does not, by any means, relieve the believer of responsibility for working out exactly what it is that he or she believes. What it does do is set the believer free to pursue that process without assuming that such a process has to be reasonably complete or watertight before participation in the life of the Church can be permitted. In other words it restores the proper balance between theology and spirituality so that prayer and worship and participation in the life of the worshipping community is understood to be part of the way in which any believer comes to formulate what it is he or she believes. There is not an initial and possibly superior rational process to be gone through before that participation can be obtained.

This rediscovery of the mystical life will also affirm that the believer is the one known rather than the knower. All the mystic writers in some sense deny that I am a self. In other words the mystical tradition finds it easier to speak of 'union', or being known by God than it does to speak of the individual 'knowing' self. This is clearly the reason why, for example, sexual imagery is prevalent among the mystical writers and, furthermore, why the new wave of postmodernist theologians have taken such an interest in what they have to say. It also places intellectual knowledge within the overall framework of the 'knowledge' brought about by love rather than assuming that love and knowledge were separate matters. A further result of the recovery of the mystical life within the Church will be a restoration of the place of happiness and freedom to act for others. Joy and freedom derive from the understanding that one is known. The result is joy and freedom for the self and freedom to act in joy for others. The person who is known by God is free to be for and with others and is *joyfully* able to be free for and with others and particularly for and with others who are marginalized, poor and the victims of others.

This means that the mystical person will become a liminal witness. *Limen* is Latin for 'threshold' or 'sill' and the contemplative person is somebody who is able, because of their interior freedom, to stand on the threshold with those who are excluded, who is able to stand and identify with those who are on the margins of society because they have a deeper freedom within themselves and do not find their authenticity or their identity given them by the establishment to which they belong. In other words, they are free within and therefore can stand on the threshold of things. And so the contemplative person will become a liminal witness able to be on the margins with the unemployed and the sick. Hermits are liminal people. Parish priests are liminal people because they are on the edge of established society. In one sense all Christians, because they exist as Christians by virtue of the mystical life which they share with God, are called to be liminal people or at the very least to be prepared to allow that witness to emerge within them whenever necessary.

The mystical life is essentially a hidden matter. It is occasionally visible but it belongs properly underground coursing along in hidden streams below the surface of our lives. It is a river deep within the rock of our lives coursing along in the dark. A hidden music. A call sign secreted into the rich and abundant scoring of the great opera of life, a tune which occasionally bursts to the surface and makes its presence known. This mystical life is secret because it is of God.

God is not seen except by his effects. He cannot be known entire. She is not experienced neat. He cannot be seen entire or all at once because she is God. To experience him neat would mean our annihilation. She simply is. And we resist this because we want to name her or to manage him or control her. But in matters of the spirit this is not possible. And that means that our language about God and our talk about God is inherently problematical and must remain so. And we must be content with that. The fault of the current Church is that it does not actually see that it is doing another thing. God is what is going on. We are part of that which is going on. God it is who constantly speaks her word and makes and then re-makes what is going on and we are that which is spoken and so made and constantly re-made. God constantly goes before us, only showing us his retreating existence and calling us to follow. God it is who constantly redeems that which we have left undone or broken.

Notes

1 'A deep but dazzling darkness'

1 Helen Waddell (tr.), *The Desert Fathers* (New York, Vintage Spiritual Classics, 1998), p. 27.
2 Waddell, *Desert Fathers*, p. 27.
3 Waddell, *Desert Fathers*, p. 28.
4 Thomas Merton, *The Wisdom of the Desert* (London, Sheldon Press, 1961), p. 3.
5 Merton, *Wisdom*, p. 23.
6 Bernard of Clairvaux, *On Loving God*, VI. 18.
7 Bernard, *On Loving God*, II. 4.
8 Henri Nouwen, *Reaching Out* (London, Collins, 1976), p. 30.
9 Thomas Merton, *Contemplative Prayer* (London, Darton, Longman & Todd, 1973), p. 26.

2 'A space within which God can act'?

1 Psalm 104.24–29 (NRSV).
2 John 9.4 (NRSV).
3 John Marsh, *The Gospel of St. John* (London, Penguin, 1968), p. 378.
4 Matthew 5.6 (NRSV).
5 Simon Tugwell OP, *Reflections on the Beatitudes* (London, Darton, Longman & Todd, 1980), p. 50.
6 Philippians 2.6–8 (NRSV).
7 Thomas Merton, *Contemplation in a World of Action* (Unwin, 1980), p. 154.

3 A Colour-Blind Church?

1 Richard Harries, *Art and the Beauty of God* (London, Mowbray, 1993), p. 5.
2 Mark McIntosh, *Mystical Theology* (Oxford, Blackwell, 1998), p. 63.
3 John Milbank, Catherine Pickstock and Graham Ward (eds), *Radical Orthodoxy* (London, Routledge, 1999), p. 1.

4 Graham Ward (ed.), *The Postmodern God* (Oxford, Blackwell, 1997), p. xxi.
5 McIntosh, *Mystical Theology*, p. 32.
6 McIntosh, *Mystical Theology*, p. x.
7 Doctrine Commission of the Church of England, *We Believe in God* (London, Church House Publishing, 1987).

4 'My Beloved Spake ...' – The Re-enchantment of the Self

1 Song of Songs 2.10–11; 3.1 (AV).
2 Bernard of Clairvaux, *Sermon on the Song of Songs*, 2.II.3, tr. G. R. Evans, Classics of Western Spirituality (New York, Paulist Press, 1987), p. 216.
3 Bernard, *Sermons*, 3.III.6, tr. Evans, 'Classics', p. 223.
4 Bernard McGinn, *The Presence of God: A History of Christian Mysticism. Vol. 2: The Growth of Mysticism* (London, SCM Press, 1994), p. 154.
5 2 Corinthians 3.18.
6 Iris Murdoch, *The Sovereignty of Good* (London, Routledge, 1970), p. 35.
7 Murdoch, *Sovereignty*, p. 34.
8 Murdoch, *Sovereignty*, p. 40.
9 Murdoch, *Sovereignty*, p. 66.
10 Hans Urs von Balthasar, *The Glory of the Lord. Vol. 1: Seeing the Form* (Edinburgh, T. & T. Clark, 1982), p. 121.
11 Hans Urs von Balthasar, *Prayer* (London, SPCK, 1973), p. 21.
12 Thomas Merton, *The New Man* (London, Burns & Oates, 1976), p. 24.
13 Thomas Merton, *Seeds of Contemplation* (Wheathampstead, Anthony Clarke Books, 1972), p. 219.
14 James Alison, *The Joy of Being Wrong* (New York, Crossroads, 1998), p. 44.
15 Alison, *Joy*, p. 45.
16 David S. Cunningham, *These Three Are One* (Oxford, Blackwell, 1998), p. 28.
17 Herbert McCabe OP, 'Aquinas on the Trinity', *New Blackfriars*, vol. 80, no. 940 (June 1999).
18 Cunningham, *These Three*, p. 220.
19 Cunningham, *These Three*, p. 189.

5 'I will give you a voice' – The Re-enchantment of Speech

1 Annie Dillard, *Teaching a Stone to Talk* (New York, Harper & Row, 1988), p. 67.
2 Exodus 20.18 (AV).
3 *The Apostolic Tradition* 35.

4 Gregory of Nazianzus, *Dogmatic Poems* (*PG* 37, pp. 507–8).
5 Ann and Barry Ulanov, *Primary Speech* (London, SCM Press, 1985), p. ix.
6 Origen, *On Prayer*, 10–11, cited by Olivier Clement, *The Roots of Christian Mysticism* (London, New City, 1993), p. 186.
7 Seamus Heaney, *The Government of the Tongue* (London, Faber, 1988), p. 107.
8 Carol Ochs, *Song of the Self* (Valley Forge PA, Trinity Press International, 1994), p. 23.
9 T. S. Eliot, *Four Quartets* (London, Faber, 1943).
10 Les Murray, *The Paperback Tree* (Manchester, Carcanet, 1992), p. 262.
11 The nearest I know is Jonathan Magonet in *Dialogue with a Difference*, ed. T. Bayfield and M. Braybrooke (London, SCM Press, 1992), where he suggests that 'higher criticism' is really a sort of 'midrash'.
12 Murray, *Tree*, p. 263.
13 Rainer Maria Rilke, *Sonnets to Orpheus* 1.7, tr. J. B. Leishman (London, Penguin, 1964).
14 Rainer Maria Rilke, *Duino Elegies* 9, tr. Stephen Mitchell (London, Picador, 1987).
15 Rilke, *Duino Elegies* 7.
16 Catherine Pickstock, *After Writing* (Oxford, Blackwell, 1998).
17 John Milbank, *The Word Made Strange* (Oxford, Blackwell, 1997), p. 2.
18 Milbank, *The Word*, p. 2.
19 George Steiner, *Real Presences* (London, Faber, 1989), p. 49.

6 'But dwelt at home ...' – The Re-enchantment of Action

1 Julie Barrett, unpublished thesis, quoted with permission.
2 Christopher Moody, *Eccentric Ministry* (London, Darton, Longman & Todd, 1992), p. 4.
3 Moody, *Ministry*, p. 5.
4 Eugene H. Peterson, *The Contemplative Pastor* (Grand Rapids MI, Eerdmans, 1989), p. 17.
5 Peterson, *Pastor*, p. 23.
6 R. E. C. Browne, *The Ministry of the Word* (London, SCM Press, 2nd edn, 1976), p. 47.
7 Geoffrey Chaucer, *The Prologue to the Canterbury Tales*, 1.480, ed. Pollard (London, Macmillan, 1953).
8 Anthony Russell, *The Country Parson* (London, SPCK, 1993), p. 230.
9 Abraham Heschel, *I Asked for Wonder*, ed. S. H. Dresner (New York, Crossroad, 1995), p. 4.
10 Michael Mayne, *This Sunrise of Wonder* (London, Fount, 1995), p. 88.
11 John Keats, Letter to George and Thomas Keats, 1817.
12 Browne, *Ministry*, p. 57.

13 Gerard Loughlin, *Telling God's Story* (Cambridge University Press 1996), p. 220.
14 Sara Maitland, *A Big-Enough God?* (London, Mowbray, 1995).
15 Maitland, *Big-Enough God?* p. 62.
16 Maitland, *Big-Enough God?* p. 231.

7 Is Mysticism an Experience?

1 Cited by John V. Taylor in *The Christlike God* (London, SCM Press, 1992).
2 Rowan Williams, 'Butler's Christian Mysticism', *Downside Review* (1984).
3 James D. G. Dunn, *The Theology of Paul the Apostle* (Edinburgh, T. & T. Clark, 1998), p. 549.
4 Grace Jantzen, *Power, Gender and Christian Mysticism* (Cambridge University Press, 1995), p. 21.
5 Jantzen, *Power*, p. 21.
6 Denys Turner, *The Darkness of God* (Cambridge University Press, 1995), p. 2.
7 Turner, *Darkness*, p. 4.
8 Jantzen, *Power*, p. 7.
9 Jantzen, *Power*, p. 3.
10 Rowan Williams, *Teresa of Avila* (London, Geoffrey Chapman, 1991), p. 147.
11 Turner, *Darkness*, p. 19.
12 Turner, *Darkness*, p. 20.
13 Psalm 139.12 (AV).

8 Mysticism and the Postmodern

1 Turner, *Darkness*, p. 5.
2 Turner, *Darkness*, p. 6.
3 Turner, *Darkness*, p. 8.
4 Turner, *Darkness*, p. 272.
5 Maitland, *Big-Enough God?* p. 103.
6 Don Cupitt, *Mysticism after Modernity* (Oxford, Blackwell, 1998), p. 5.
7 Cupitt, *Mysticism*, p. 8.
8 Cupitt, *Mysticism*, p. 99.
9 Cupitt, *Mysticism*, p. 104.
10 Cupitt, *Mysticism*, p. 113.
11 Cupitt, *Mysticism*, p. 108.
12 Cupitt, *Mysticism*, p. 97.
13 Denys Turner, 'Cupitt, the mystics and the "objectivity" of God' in Colin Crowder (ed.), *God and Reality* (London, Mowbray, 1997), p. 119.
14 Turner, 'Cupitt', p. 124.

15 Turner, 'Cupitt', p. 125.
16 Cupitt, *Mysticism*, p. 128.
17 Meister Eckhart, *The Essential Sermons, Commentaries, Treatises and Defense*, ed. Edmund Colledge OSA and Bernard McGinn (London, SPCK, 1981), Sermon 83, p. 208.
18 Eckhart, *Essential Sermons*, Sermon 5b, p. 183.
19 Turner, 'Cupitt', p. 126.

9 The Affirmative Way

1 Thomas Merton, *Conjectures of a Guilty Bystander* (London, Sheldon Press, 1977), p. 217.
2 Pseudo-Dionysius, *Letters*, 9.5, cited by Bernard McGinn, *The Foundations of Christian Mysticism* (London, SCM Press, 1991).
3 Pseudo-Dionysius, *Divine Names*, 4.13, cited by McGinn, *Foundations*.
4 Meister Eckhart, *Commentary on Exodus*, para 16, in *Meister Eckhart, Teacher and Preacher*, ed. Bernard McGinn, Classics of Western Spirituality (New York, Paulist Press, 1996), p. 46.
5 Origen, *Commentary on the Song of Songs*, Prologue, cited by McGinn, *Foundations*.
6 Origen, *Song of Songs*, Book 1, cited by McGinn, *Foundations*.
7 See, among others, Renita J. Weems in the *New Interpreter's Bible*, vol. 5 (Nashville, Abingdon Press, 1997).
8 Cited by McGinn, *Foundations*, p. 119.
9 Denys Turner, *Eros and Allegory* (Kalamazoo, Cistercian Publications, 1995), p. 79.
10 Bernard of Clairvaux, *Sermons on the Song of Songs*, 79.
11 Thomas Traherne, *Desire*, in *Selected Writings*, ed. D. Davis (Manchester, Carcanet, 1988).
12 Thomas Traherne, *Centuries of Meditations*. 1.42, ed. B. Dobell (London, P. and A. Dobell, 1927).
13 Traherne, *Centuries*, 1.44.
14 Philip Sheldrake, *Befriending Our Desires* (London, Darton, Longman & Todd, 1994), p. 22.
15 Traherne, *Centuries*, 3.3.
16 Maitland, *Big-Enough God?* p. 50.
17 Annie Dillard, *Pilgrim at Tinker Creek* (New York, Harper & Row, 1974), p. 204.
18 Dillard, *Pilgrim*, p. 30.
19 Dillard, *Pilgrim*, p. 30.
20 Dillard, *Pilgrim*, p. 270.
21 Dillard, *Pilgrim*, p. 146.

10 The Negative Way

1 John of the Cross, *Dark Night of the Soul*, 2.5.3, in St John of the Cross, *Selected Writings*, ed. Kieran Kavanagh OCD, Classics of Western Spirituality (New York, Paulist Press, 1987), p. 201.

2 Exodus 33.20–23.

3 Gregory of Nyssa, *The Life of Moses*, para 232, tr. Abraham J. Malherbe and Everett Ferguson, Classics of Western Spirituality (New York, Paulist Press, 1978), p. 115.

4 Gregory of Nyssa, *Life of Moses*, para. 163.

5 *The Cloud of Unknowing*, ch. 1, ed. James Walsh SJ, Classics of Western Spirituality (New York, Paulist Press, 1981), p. 116.

6 *Cloud*, ch. 3.

7 *Cloud*, ch. 1.

8 John of the Cross, *The Spiritual Canticle*, 14/15.15, 'Classics', p. 249.

9 John of the Cross, *Spiritual Canticle*, 14/15.16, p. 250.

10 *Cloud*, ch. 4.

11 Andrew Louth, *The Origins of the Christian Mystical Tradition* (Oxford, Clarendon Press, 1981), p. 200.

12 McGinn, *Foundations*, p. 170.

13 *Cloud*, Prologue.

14 Turner, *Darkness*, p. 39.

15 Turner, *Darkness*, p. 26.

16 Merton, *Seeds*, p. 220.

17 Merton, *Seeds*, p. 221.

18 Meister Eckhart, German Sermons 5b, 'In hoc apparuit charitas dei in nobis', *Essential Sermons*, p. 183.

19 Turner, *Darkness*, p. 244.

20 Emily Dickinson, 'This World is not Conclusion'. There are a number of editions of Emily Dickinson's poetry; see *A Choice of Emily Dickinson's Verse*, selected by Ted Hughes (London, Faber, 1968).

21 R. S. Thomas, *Counterpoint* (Newcastle upon Tyne, Bloodaxe Books, 1990), p. 54.

22 David Scott, *Parson Poets of the West Country*, unpublished.

23 Paul Celan, *Psalm*, tr. John Felstiner in John Felstiner, *Paul Celan: Poet, Survivor, Jew* (New Haven, Yale University Press, 1995), p. 167.

24 Felstiner, *Paul Celan*, p. 168.

25 Celan, *Mandorla*, tr. Felstiner, p. 180.

26 Scott, *Parson Poets*.

Index

The Society for Promoting Christian Knowledge (SPCK) was founded in 1698. Its mission statement is:

To promote Christian knowledge by

- **Communicating the Christian faith in its rich diversity**
- **Helping people to understand the Christian faith and to develop their personal faith; and**
- **Equipping Christians for mission and ministry**

SPCK Worldwide serves the Church through Christian literature and communication projects in 100 countries, and provides books for those training for ministry in many parts of the developing world. This worldwide service depends upon the generosity of others and all gifts are spent wholly on ministry programmes, without deductions.

SPCK Bookshops support the life of the Christian community by making available a full range of Christian literature and other resources, providing support for those training for ministry, and assisting bookstalls and book agents throughout the UK.

SPCK Publishing produces Christian books and resources, covering a wide range of inspirational, pastoral, practical and academic subjects. Authors are drawn from many different Christian traditions, and publications aim to meet the needs of a wide variety of readers in the UK and throughout the world.

The Society does not necessarily endorse the individual views contained in its publications, but hopes they stimulate readers to think about and further develop their Christian faith.

For information about the Society, visit our website at
www.spck.org.uk, or write to:
SPCK, Holy Trinity Church, Marylebone Road,
London NW1 4DU, United Kingdom.